TAROT FOR BEGINNERS:

A Modern Guide to the Cards, Spreads, and Revealing the Mystery of the Tarot

Maria Butfield

© **Copyright 2020 by Maria Butfield
All rights reserved.**

This document is geared towards providing exact and reliable information in regards to the topic and issue covered. The publication is sold with the idea that the publisher is not required to render accounting, officially permitted, or otherwise, qualified services. If advice is necessary, legal or professional, a practiced individual in the profession should be ordered.

- From a Declaration of Principles which was accepted and approved equally by a Committee of the American Bar Association and a Committee of Publishers and Associations.

In no way is it legal to reproduce, duplicate, or transmit any part of this document in either electronic means or in printed format. Recording of this publication is strictly prohibited and any storage of this document is not allowed unless with written permission from the publisher. All rights reserved.

The information provided herein is stated to be truthful and consistent, in that any liability, in terms of inattention or otherwise, by any usage or abuse of any policies, processes, or directions contained within is the solitary and utter responsibility of the recipient reader. Under no circumstances will any legal responsibility or blame be held against the publisher for any reparation, damages, or monetary loss due to the information herein, either directly or indirectly.

Respective authors own all copyrights not held by the publisher.

The information herein is offered for informational purposes solely, and is universal as so. The presentation of the information is without contract or any type of guarantee assurance.

The trademarks that are used are without any consent, and the publication of the trademark is without permission or backing by the trademark owner. All trademarks and brands within this book are for clarifying purposes only and are the owned by the owners themselves, not affiliated with this document.

Table of Content

Introduction 1

Part 1: Origin and History of Tarot Cards 4

1.1 The Hermetic Order of Golden Dawn 5

1.2 Esotericism 12

1.3 Psychics and Tarot Cards 19

1.4 The Church and the Tarot Cards 22

Part 2: Reading of Tarot Cards 30

2.1 Importance of Sacred Place for Reading Cards . 31

2.2 Things You Must Consider While Choosing Your Deck 35

2.3 Preparing for Tarot Reading 41

2.4 The Layout of the Cards 46

2.5 Reading Tarot for Yourself 64

2.6 How to Clean Tarot Decks? 74

Part 3: Interpretation of Tarot Cards and their Meaning 84

3.1 The Major Arcana 86

3.2 The Minor Arcana 105

3.3 Trusting Your Intuition 144

3.4 Combination of Cards 149

3.5 The Meaning of Numbers and Colors in Tarot World 158

3.6 Which Tarot Cards Are Considered Good? 164

3.7 Reading of Reversed Tarot Cards and Their Meanings 176

Part 4: Curiosity 193

4.1 Numerology and Tarot Cards 193

4.2 Astrology and Tarot Cards 194

Conclusion 206

References 208

Introduction

Playing cards is considered a fun game and is full of thrill. The cards are not only fantastic for the playing purpose only but also are used for fortune-telling, love scrolling, relationship, finance and job-related things. I am talking about tarot cards, that have been used from the ancient times with different faiths by different religions people. Even in this modern era, yet the tarot cards are playing a significant role in life with pocket-full of earnings. There are different layouts of tarots. These include Three card reading, seven horseshoe spread, spiritual spread, astrological spread or Celtic Cross spread etc.

You can read tarot cards for yourself as well for others. There are some necessities for reading tarots and choosing a sacred space is one of the most important things. Then you select a deck and keep it clean. Tarot deck consist of 78 total cards, of which twenty-two are major arcana cards, and fifty-six are minor arcana cards. They are then further broken down into four suits. Tarot card four suits have cups, pentacles, wands, and swords. Each suite is equipped with four court cards: page, knight, queen and king. There is also one ace card in each suit and nine pip cards numbered from two to 10. There are different symbols attached to each card, that shows some hint about your life. This hint might be from the past event, your present condition, or your coming days' targets. These cards will tell you that either you are on the right track or should you continue the way you are dealing with the things or change it. Trusting your intuition while reading tarots is the most crucial factor for a successful reading. You can also read a different combination of cards, for example, the Sun and the Magician. Every number of the card has a different meaning, just like every color has a different meaning in the tarot world. I mean there is a relationship between Numerology and tarots. You can also see a connection between Astrology and tarots like how earth, water, fire and air are related to tarot cards. So, we can say there is a connection between the planets and the tarots. No matter for which area of life you are concerned about the tarot cards, trust in your gut and stay positive to get the positive outcome.

Part 1: Origin and History of Tarot Cards

Tarot readings are a powerful technique of divination that uses an ancient card deck to help you find answers to your most prominent concerns like love, relationships, job, finances, and more. For hundreds of years, psychics and fortune tellers have used Tarot cards, and Trusted Tarot could give you an accurate reading that is customized based on the cards you select and the order you choose them. Depending on their position, every card has a different sense so that you can get a unique and comprehensive perspective on your current situation. The things I am going to discuss regarding tarot reading will be beneficial for you, but before moving forward, isn't it better to discuss some history of tarot cards.

Since ancient times human beings have used tarot cards. It was noted that the Egyptians used glass-like disks that resembled playing card decks, while medieval Europe gypsies often used cards that depicted various colorful drawings on them. The tarot's first-ever documented use in Europe was in 1375, and travelling Islamic clerks and societies are thought to introduce it to the mainland. Tarot cards were called tarocchi, trionfi and tarock cards in the mid-15th century. Card patterns ranged across Europe as did the suits. However, each deck had four suits which consisted of 14 cards. Every suit had ten pip cards numbered 10 to one or 10 to two with an ace acting like one. There were four face-cards in all the four suits: a king, a queen, a knight, a jack, and a page. Also, in parts of Europe, modern tarot cards are still used as cards for playing games such as French Tarot and Italian tarocchini. Tarot cards are however used almost exclusively for divination in English-speaking countries.

1.1 The Hermetic Order of Golden Dawn

The primary goal and aim of Magic's Golden Dawn scheme is the emergence into full consciousness of the Divine Spark that is present within each of us, stifled by contemporary education and sensory-reliant life-experience. Magicians try to complete their life-long energetic evolution. The Golden Dawn Hermetic Order is one of the most prominent mystic western societies of the late 19th to early 20th century. It exploded into the light like a comet, blazed a bright path and then disintegrated. Members included W. B. Yeats, A. E. Waite, Aleister Crowley, among others. Dr William Wynn Westcott, a London coroner and a rosicrucian, was the central founder of the Golden Dawn.

In 1887 Westcott got from the rev. Part of a document written in brown-ink cipher A. F. A. Mason Woodford. The manuscript looked aged but was not. It is assumed Westcott is the author himself. Westcott believed he could decode the text and found that it contained fragments of "Golden Dawn" rites, an obscure group that supposedly accepted both men and women. Westcott asked Samuel Liddell MacGregor Mathers, an occult acquaintance, to flesh out the fragments into rituals of full scale. Such papers were fabricated to give authenticity and history to the "Golden

Dawn." It was claimed to be an Old Occult German order. Westcott produced documents to show that he had been granted a charter for creating an independent lodge in England.

The Isis-Urania Temple of the Golden Dawn Hermetic Order was founded in 1888 with the three members being Westcott, Mathers, and Dr W. R. Woodman, Supreme Magus of the Anglia Rosicrucian Society. The secret society quickly caught on, and during the heydey of the society, three hundred and fifteen initiations took place, from 1888 to 1896. An elaborate hierarchy was created that consisted of 10 grades or degrees, each corresponding to the Kabbalah's Tree of Life's ten sephiroth, plus the 11th grade for neophytes. Divide the degrees into three orders: Outer, Second, and Third.

Another progressed by Inspection by the Outer Order. Initially, Westcott, Mathers, and Woodman were the only members of the Second Order, claiming to be under the guidance of the Third Order Secret Chiefs, who were astral plane entities. The practices of Mathers were primarily based on the Freemasonry. Woodman died in 1891 in the company and was not replaced. Mathers created the initiation rite for the minor rank of Adeptus and called the Second Order of the Ordo Rosae Rubeae et Aureae Crucis or the Rose and Gold Cross Order. Initiation was only by invitation. Mathers was at least unstable and was probably mentally ill. His wife, Mina, who, he said, received instructions from the Secret Chiefs through clairaudience or supernormal vision, never consummated his marriage. His finances were volatile, and he and his wife became penniless in 1891.

Annie Horniman, a wealthy Golden Dawner, had been their benefactor. Mathers moved to Paris with his wife, where Mathers founded another lodge. He kept writing materials for the curricula and submitting them to London. He was fascinated with Westcott's envy and became even more autocratic. He devoted much of time to translate the manuscript of Abra-Melin the Mage's The Book of the Sacred Magic which he believed was enchanted and inhabited by a nonphysical intelligence species. (The book was finally published in 1898). Horniman cut off its financial assistance to Mathers in 1896. The same year Mathers said he had been welcomed into the Third Order by the Secret Chiefs. Horniman disputed his assertion and was evicted from society. Members started to discover the dubious role of Westcott in 'discovering' the Golden Dawn in 1897. He had resigned his post, and Florence Farr replaced him.

By then, within the Golden Dawn, irreparable schisms had formed. In 1898, Aleister Crowley was introduced, and the ranks rapidly grew. He went to Paris in 1899 and demanded that he be accepted into the Second Order. Mathers obeyed. Under Farr, the London lodge refused his initiation. In 1900 Crowley went to England as "Envoy Extraordinary" of Mathers and sought to take charge of the Second Order rooms.

He emerged wearing a black mask, a Highland dress and a golden knife, storming the lodge before turning away. Alliance with the Crowley-Mathers has also been troubled. Crowley found Mathers to be a superior magician. The two reportedly fought supernatural warfare. Mathers sent an astral vampire to psychologically attack Crowley, and Crowley replied with a Beelzebub-led army of Demons.

Both Crowley and Mathers were removed from London lodge. Crowley retaliated by publishing in his journal, The Equinox, certain secret rituals of the Golden Dawn. W. B. Yeats believed the Second Class. He sought to restore unity, but the Golden Dawn schisms split into separate parties. Mathers followers founded the Temple of Alpha et Omega. During 1903 A. E. Waite and others quit, forming a community called Golden Dawn but with a focus on mysticism rather than magic. Another splinter group, the Stella matutina, or "Call of the Companions of the rising Light in the morning," was founded in 1905. Isis-Uranian Temple was departed. In 1917 it was revived as the Stella matutina merlin shrine. The Stella matutina declined in the 1940s, after a former member, Israel Regardie, Crowley's one-time secretary, revealed its inner rituals. Waite's party, which retained the name Golden Dawn and some of its traditions, declined with Waite's departure after 1915. Some remote Golden Dawn offshoots remain in existence. During its height, the Golden Dawn Hermetic Order possessed the largest known archive of magical Western knowledge. Research of the Second Order based on the kabbalistic Tree of Life.

They taught three magical systems: Solomon's principal (see grimoires); Abramelin's magic (see Abramelin the mage); and Enochian magic (see John Dee). Materials were also adapted from the Book of the Deads of Egypt, the Prophecy Books of William Blake and the Chaldean Oracles. Instruction in astral travel, scrying, alchemy, geomancy, the tarot, and astrology was given. The main aim of the order was to "pursue the Great Work: to get control over the essence and influence of [one's] own being." Some of the texts contained Christian elements, such as having a closer relationship with Jesus, the "master of masters." Members circulated numerous Catholic and Anglican writings and sermons. These were removed from Regardie's written materials.

Elements of Golden Dawn practices, rosicrucianism, and Freemasonry were incorporated into modern Witchcraft practices.

1.2 Esotericism

Esotericism applies to the doctrines or practices of occult wisdom, or the mysterious nature or state. Esoteric knowledge is specialized or advanced in nature, only available to a narrow circle of "enlightened," "initiated," or highly educated individuals. Esoteric knowledge is usually contrasted with exoteric knowledge, which is well-known or regarded by the public as being informally normative across society. Items that relate to esotericism may be called esoterics. Esotericism generally requires an initiation dimension such as the requirement that one be checked before the higher truth is discovered. Such knowledge may, however, be kept secret not by the intention of its protectors, but by its very nature — for example, if it is only accessible to those with a proper intellectual background. There may be some similarities between esotericism and mysticism. Still, many mystical traditions do not try to incorporate additional divine insight, but instead, aim to concentrate the attention or prayers of the practitioner more firmly on the object of devotion. Therefore, a mystic isn't inherently esotericist. Because of their "inner" emphasis as well as their "selective" and "secretive" nature, several past practices may be identified as types of "esotericism."

Esotericism is not a single practice but a vast array of figures and movements often unrelated. Nevertheless, the following examples provide an overview of some of the most famous mystical movements and characters throughout history. In the ancient Graeco-Roman world, "mystery religions," or only "mysteries," were systems of belief in which complete membership was limited to those who had gone through certain secret rites of initiation." In this sense, the word "mystery" derives from the Latin mystery, from the Greek musterion, meaning "secret rite or doctrine." A person who followed such a mystery was a mystery, "one who was initiated," from myein, "to close, shut," perhaps a reference to secrecy, or was permitted to observe and participate in rituals only by initiates.

Therefore, the Mysteries were belief structures in which all religious activities were inaccessible to the non-induced, and for which the general public kept secret the inner workings of faith. While there are no other specific requirements, the lack of an ideology and scripture have characterized mystery religions. Through nature, sects practiced in secret only to escape religious persecution are not mysteries. Also retained in the term "mystery play" is the old sense of "mystery." These stage plays of medieval Europe were regarded as such because the first groups to perform them were the guilds of craftsmen, whose membership involved initiation and who fiercely protected their trade secrets.

The Mysteries are frequently confused with Gnosticism, perhaps in part because Greek gnosis means "intelligence." However, the gnosis of Gnosticism is distinct from the Arcanum, the "true wisdom" of the Mysteries: while the Gnostics hoped to gain knowledge through divine revelation, the religions of the mystery presumed to have it, with mysteries of high rank revealing to the acolytes of l the possessed wisdom. The word "mystery religion" refers to some of the many belief systems of the late classical antiquity the eastern Mediterranean including the Eleusinian Mysteries, the Orphic Mysteries, and the Mithraic Mysteries. Many of the other deities that the Romans nominally adopted from other civilizations, such as the Egyptian Isis, the Thracian/Phrygian Sabazius and the Phrygian Cybele, also came to be worshipped in Mysteries.

"Plato, the member of one of these holy orders, was harshly criticized because he exposed many of the hidden theological concepts of the Mysteries to the public in his writings" (Hall). The religions of mystery are perhaps one of the roots of Western mystery culture, but the two must not be confused with each other. Since Christianity became Rome's official religion, Christian dissident groups were marginalized as Official traitors. Pagan parties also came in for repression. The words "Gnosticism" and "Gnosis" were disputed as specific concepts, but refer to a family of ancient Jewish, Christian, and pagan religious movements that frequently claimed to have hidden messages about the spirit world as opposed to the everyday world they appeared to denigrate. The notable shift from the ancient world was Hermeticism, often called Hermetism to differentiate it from its post-Renaissance appropriations. Ancient Babylon independently laid the groundwork for Western astrology. Some see Christianity, with its baptismal rite, as a religion of mystery.

In the Middle Ages, things like astrology, alchemy, and sorcery were not removed from the normal subjects of a learned person's curriculum. Although some believe esotericism is contrary to the Bible or Christianity, this conflict did not emerge until later as a historical matter. Christianity contributed its mystic imagery, especially the Holy Grail from Arthurian literature. Although specific esoteric topics have thousands of years of history, these have typically not survived as ongoing practices. Instead, complex antique revival movements have benefited from them. For example, during the Italian Renaissance, translators such as Ficino and Pico dells Mirandola turned their attention to Neo-Platonism's classical literature, and what was considered to be the pre-Mosaic tradition of Hermeticism.

In the seventeenth century European esotericism was reformulated as Rosicrucianism, and subsequently joined various branches of Freemasonry. A prominent French revival in turn, in the nineteenth century, gave way to H's Theosophy. And P. Blavatsky. In the twenty-first century Annie Besant, C. W. Leadbeater, Alice Bailey, Rudolf Steiner and many others reformulated Theosophy. Theosophy is also considered a significant force in philosophical societies, "Ascended Master Practices," and within the New Age groups, on the many present varieties of esotericism. Yet another significant mystic variation stems from G's teachings. Gurdjieff I. P. Ouspensky, D. Rudolf Steiner, who broke with Theosophy to found his anthroposophy, spoke at the nineteenth century's end, of a disagreement between esotericists. It was because one branch wanted to open esoteric knowledge to the general public, while another group wanted to maintain secrecy. Steiner himself claimed to be in the lineage of those who tried to make esoteric a part of the mainstream acceptance. His first writings, published in the 19th century, resisted any reference to religious concepts. Still, he found the 20th century as the dawn of a new era, when spirituality would become increasingly important to human development. Therefore, he began publishing works such as Theosophy and Occult Science and lecturing on occult subjects for both the collection of audiences (members of the Anthroposophical Society or his mystical school) and the public. All of his writings but the most esoteric of these lectures have been published throughout his lifetime. Even the most esoteric material has been made available by the Rudolf Steiner Archive. In contemporary English use, the word "esoteric" in the sense of "hidden" intelligence, traditions, or practices especially does not apply to "esotericism" per se. The word "esotericism" has come to mean informally any knowledge that is hard to understand or recall, such as abstract physics, or anything relating to a specific discipline's minutiae, such as "esoteric" baseball statistics.

1.3 Psychics and Tarot Cards

Psychics and tarot cards are like strawberries and cream, and they go together. Why? For what? It hardly makes sense when you think about it, psychics have been around since the first person thought there was such a thing as 'later,' tarot cards on the other hand, at least in their current form, only dating back to the middle of the 15th century. We must get to the heart of what a psychic is and get to the bottom of the mystery. If you were to survey what 'psychic' means to people, they'd probably come up with the picture of a woman covered in scarves and dripping with bangles staring into a crystal ball with kohled eyes.

The truth is a little different. A psychic is a person who, without using the standard five senses of sight, touch, taste or smell, can access knowledge. Such a person tends to use other abilities to acquire information, such as clairvoyance, insight, or mediumship, and how they use this information varies as well. A psychic, for example, can solve crimes, expel unwanted energies, or act as a medium; as a medium once explained to me, all mediums are psychic, but not all psychics are media. Among occultists, the general belief is that almost everybody is psychic: just as most people can walk. However, that doesn't mean everyone is as psychic as everyone else. Think about it like this: most people can walk; some can walk very fast or for long distances and then there's Usain Bolt – the distinction is a mix of natural talent, plenty of hard work and practice. Now, Mr. Bolt isn't just taking any pair of shoes and going for a run, his running shoes are different, they're built to help him hit the peak of his ability, and tarot cards are a little like that. They are attractive pictures on their own, in the hands of someone psychic but not used to using them. They are beautiful pictures that can often be useful, used by a psychic who is used to using them and who is willing to practice improving their abilities, they are a fantastic tool to help the subject enhance their self-development.

Now, as we have observed almost everyone has some psychic ability, this can only be noticed very intermittently for some folk, e.g. the person who has never shown any psychic gifts before refusing to get into the car just to find out that the brakes have been broken. Others may get more frequent moments of spiritual insight, recognizing who is calling before picking up the ringing phone. Likewise, likely, someone is so psychically 'open' that they are bombarded with knowledge and fail to sort out the trees from the metaphysical wood. Imagine being on a crowded bus and being blasted with all the people's emotions on it, and it is enough to give you a headache. The trouble with these cases is that when and when they happen, the 'psychic' has no power over them.

Neither psychic appears to be able to work 100 percent of the time accurately (much to the amusement of the medical community), but with practice and other resources, they can develop and monitor their abilities, which is where tarot cards come in. The theory is that the psychic can shift their consciousness by using such techniques in such a manner that they can settle into the problem at hand without picking up on anything around them. It could mean lighting candles in the case of a tarot reader, or something as easy as taking a few quiet moments before reading to calm their minds, merely shuffling the cards and remembering the problem at hand can be enough to establish that particular state of mind. Then, looking at the images on the cards will free their imagination by giving them a story they can give to the reading subject. That is why it can be futile to study the meaning of the cards continually; relying on recalled card meanings can stifle the creative process through which insight thrives. In theory, a psychic can use anything from the flight of birds to the patterns they see in a fire to refine their abilities, but tarot cards are more realistic, built for the job and don't risk burning down your home in the process.

1.4 The Church and the Tarot Cards

Tarot's been through several reinventions over time. The method of divination has many theories of creation, has discussed history and philosophy. What once was a game of cards has gradually developed into today's most common divination method. It was given more mystical influence and more profound meaning as it passed through the hands of Antoine Court de Gebelin in the 1780s. It again repeated as the method went through Etteilla's hands in the 1790s, Levi in the 1850s, Mathers in the 1880s, Waite in the 1910s, Case in the 1910s, Hall in the 1920s, and finally Crowley in the 1940s. -- occultist introduced new layers of significance and impregnated them with their view of the Mysteries, making the scheme as productive as it is today in symbolism and associations. And the Medieval Church's earlier Christian faith is typically swept under the rug. While I am not a Christian, I do find the early symbolism fascinating to see how much impact it has on our modern decks. The correct claim we have is that the cards originated as Trionfi, the Italian card game, which is the root of both the tarot and our current play cards. Trionfi means "Triumph" and eventually the term "Trump" originated in card games. The Trump cards were power ranking cards, so a higher ranked card will "triumph" or "trump" cards lower than that. To understand the Trump cards and why these symbols were used, we must know when they were made, or at least popularized, which was in Renaissance Italy during the Middle Ages of the 15th Century.

In these days' triumph parades have become a familiar pageant spectacle on the streets. They were Victory floats. In Tarot Triumphs, Cherry Gilchrist wrote, "These parade triumphs showed earthly, spiritual, and religious emblems drawing on their ideals from allegory, history, and Christian teachings. A Triumph procession is represented in Petrarch's work I Trionfi, dating back to the late fourteenth century, which alludes to vices and virtues and draws from traditional symbolism in portraying the characters involved in the procession. "The Tarot Trumps, which developed into what we call the Major Arcana, displayed spiritual messages linked to God's might. The only card that refused to obey the Trump rules was The Fool card, which was the Joker's root in the tarot. The Fool card permitted the player to break the rules and not follow them, just as the court jester was able to violate laws that nobody else in the feudal system was able to do.

The Juggler (Trump 1) had more similarities to a stage magician. Anyone who used subtle tricks to impress the average citizen but diverted himself from the Church's moral values.

The Popess (Trump 2) was based on a fictional woman called Pope Joan, who fooled the Church into believing she was male and ascended to the papacy. She, sadly, when it was discovered she was a woman, was killed horribly. So she had the Juggler's trickery, but at least she did otherwise work within the context of the Church's teachings.

The Empress (Trump 3) was lower in Trumps' power because she was still female, but at least had "legitimate influence" in people's eyes, but even less control than the Emperor (Trump 4) who overshadowed her. Both reflected authority and land control.

The Male Pope was the Hierophant (Trump 5). His divine supremacy as a representative of God on earth and of the Church gave him more authority than the Empress and Emperor, for the rule of heaven was higher than the control of the world.

Next comes The Lovers (Trump 6), which was the statement by Christ that passion was the highest law.

The next collection of cards is highly inspired by the writings of Thomas Aquinas, whom Plato had a profound influence on. Though the next set of cards interject their ranks of strength, the virtues are still there. In Tarot Beyond the Basics, Anthony Louis writes that "Aquinas regarded Prudence as 'the origin, measure, and form of all virtues ... the Auriga virtue or the charioteer of virtues.'" Thus our first virtue is Prudence, symbolized by The Chariot (Trump 7) which opened the way for its other virtues, Justice (Trump 8), Fortitude as Strength (Trump 11), and Temperance (Trump 14). The Hermit (Trump 9) lived a monk's life observing the virtues and leading a life of prayer, reflection and introspection.

The Wheel of Fortune (Trump 10) portrayed things beyond our control, things entrusted to the stars and God. The Hanged Man (Trump 12) represented both the submission to God and the death of Christ hanging upon the cross, who himself surrendered as the death of God's will. Then comes Death (Trump 13), to whom we will all surrender in, whether we are a Hermit, a King, a Juggler, a Fool, or a Hierophant.

The Devil (Trump 15) is also a clear sign of Christianity, reflecting the things that lure us away from salvation. The Devil is in his control beyond life and death. He is referred to in the Bible as the "Angel of the earth." The Tower (Trump 16) is the Babel Tower struck down by Satan, reflecting the power of the Devil is making people believe they can conquer Satan through their greed.

The Star (Trump 17) is Bethlehem's Star which heralds a sign of hope for Christ's birth so that people can be saved.

The Moon (Trump 18) depicts the Virgin Mary who is also depicted with celestial imagery and will give origin to The Sun (Trump 19), which shows the Child of Christ, the light of the earth.

Following this, we have Judgment (Trump 20), referring to the last Judgment following Armageddon, as Jesus returns to judge the souls of the deceased that were "sleeping" in their graves—followed by The Planet (Trump 21) that reflects the New Jerusalem to be built later, the New Eden.

Tarot cards are one of the popular ways of potential reading. Being one of the most popular fortune-telling techniques in the West, they are blessed alongside crystal ball reading and palmistry, or palm reading. Traditional tarot cards have 78 cards divided into two main arcana categories, meaning "cover." Major arcana cards are twenty-two in number while there are 56 minor arcana cards. They are then further broken down into four suits. Tarot card four suits have cups, pentacles, wands, and swords. Each suite is equipped with four court cards: page, knight, queen and king. There is also one ace card in each suit and nine pip cards numbered from two to 10.

This setup sounds very familiar to anyone who plays modern card games. A deck of cards divided into four different suits, each with an ace, nine numerated cards and some face cards. Although Pages do not exist in modern playing cards, the king and queen remain, and the modern jack card may be the tarot knight's replacement. The resemblance between the ancient tarot deck and the current card-playing deck is surprising. That is how they initially used tarot cards as playing cards. After knowledge of background, our main concern will remain on tarot reading, so keep reading.

Part 2: Reading of Tarot Cards

Tarot reading is spiritual, and all readers of the tarot card stress a few simple rules to follow to obtain to attain the level of spiritual enlightenment necessary for a downright good experience. Choosing a perfect set of the tarot deck that binds to your inner soul is a big move for beginning a reading of a tarot card. Another is to create a sacred space that helps you to centralize your energies. It clears your chakras of negative influences for an interpretation of the tarot. Anything you put up for a tarot reading in your sacred room, has various impacts on you and your reading. The shades, the candles, the crystals, the light, the sound, all the little things that make you feel connected to your inner spirituality are significant. A space-cleaning practice is essential when you're preparing for a reading. It is not only to respect the tradition your part of as a tarot reader, but also to neutralize the energy of a room so that you, or the person you're reading for, won't be disturbed by any residual energy in the room. A read will subtract from residual energy.

2.1 Importance of Sacred Place for Reading Cards

The space in which you are reading tarot cards plays a significant role in your readings as this space helps to build confidence between you and your client. It is enabling the free flow of energy between you and your client in the reading for in-depth perception and insight. The importance of sacred space is to point to a safe physical space for reading tarot. It's a place where you put your physical, mental, emotional, and spiritual resources together to provide your client with a positive experience. After all, this is what creates their faith in you as a reader. Everybody gets a tarot card reading at open booths for infests or events at least once in their lifetime experience, and you need to learn the difference between reading in a private space versus a public space where so many people and noisy noises surround you. Every one of you, therefore, prefers to get your reading in a private room. Nevertheless, a sacred space should not be contained to the walls of a house or office, and it can also be in open spaces such as a garden or terrace, whatever makes the reader feel linked with their inner selves.

How Should Be Your Sacred Place for Tarot Cards Reading?

The sacred space must contain these things:

It should be Letting Your Spirit Flow Without any Disturbance for Tarot Reading

Physical space involves the material items like furniture, the bed, the place where the tarot cards are spread, and the various things you hold in your private space that affect the space setting. This physical space should be such that for uninterrupted readings, it provides a private atmosphere so that the reader can concentrate on reading. Such a room is not generally within the boundaries of closed walls; it may be in an open garden, a pool-side room, or on the terrace. The critical thing that matters here is unperturbed the reading area.

This space should Allow your Mind to Clear the Distractions and Focus on the Readings

Only having a private and enclosed physical space does not guarantee the experience of reading a sacred tarot. But the thing significantly affects is that the mind of the reader is free from other distractions such as their household work or other emotions that make you feel frustrated. Sacred mental space is allowing the reader to concentrate all his attention on the client's issue and provide clear insights to them.

Space should be Sensitive for Tarot Reading

The sacred space for tarot reading should be composed of various elements that help the reader clear from their minds all the negative thoughts. The items that help you balance the energies on the table are candles, crystals, music, water, and salt. In a tarot card reading, the various colors of the candles and lighting in the room carry different types of energy. These will then be chosen by the tarot card reader itself, based on the relationship that they feel with a particular candle color. For example- blue color brings peace and prosperity, and white color candles help cleanse and purify the atmosphere, Purple color strengthens the reader's mental ability and spiritual awakening, red color symbolizes passion. Most readers like to hold crystals that make them feel their inner spiritual connection. For removing the negative energies from the mind of the reader, elements of salt or salt should be included in the reading room.

The Environment Should Stimulate Your Psychic Energies

Readers believe in fostering all the four elements in the reading space that make up the Universe- Earth, Water, Fire, and Air. These elements allow them to feel the relation with and intuition of the spiritual universe. These four elements influence human emotions and can prove helpful in regulating the reader's emotions by inculcating all these elements to focus their attention on their inner wisdom.

Space should Connect you with Your Spiritual Self by Clearing our Chakras

Meditating before and after each reading is a ritual that should be practiced by all tarot card readers to clear the chakras and communicate with the spiritual forces. Chakras are the body's energy centers, and to cleanse and motivate the chakras will improve the reader's vision and inner wisdom to encourage in-depth readings.

2.2 Things You Must Consider While Choosing Your Deck

Whether you are a newcomer of Tarot or a professional practitioner, it can be tough to select a Tarot deck. There are lots of different Tarot decks to choose from, all with their meaning, strength, tales, mythology, and artwork. Where do you start, then? How do you find the dream Tarot Deck through the overwhelming array of choices?

Look for an Intuitive and Personal Interaction with the Cards

The absolute number 1 way of selecting a Tarot Deck is to choose one with which you interact personally and intuitively. Your best friend may be raving about the Crazy Unknown Deck, but if you break out in a sweat and blank every time you go to do a Tarot reading with those cards, that's not the right Deck for you. So if the Rider Waite deck swears your Tarot instructor, but you're entirely in love with the Fairy Tarot Cards, then go for the Fairy Tarot Cards. If you have a new age shop or local bookstore, go to the store and manage all the Tarot decks that are on display. What energy are you getting from the Deck? Is there a personal link between the Tarot cards and yourself? So if you are looking to buy your Tarot cards online, do a fast Google search, so browse at the photos of your card to see if you have a connection. So, Start with the intuition!

Consider Your Experience Level

If you're new to Tarot, you can prefer to start learning with the Rider Waite Deck, the most common Tarot deck. It's simple to understand, the picture is clear and realistic, and for this Deck, there's a tremendous amount of detail. Or you might choose a deck with simple, minimalist images such as the Everyday Tarot Deck for a secure link to the symbols. On the flipside, whether you're more seasoned or you're looking for a new challenge, then for its difficulty and scope, you can select a deck like the Thoth Tarot deck. Perhaps a more abstract, mystical Tarot deck close to the Tarot Shadow scapes. Of course, don't be restricted by assuming that you can only read with the Rider Waite deck while you're new to the Tarot. If you have a personal link to the cards, you do need to remember.

Decide Either You Want to Go Traditional or Modern

Are you intrigued by classic, traditional Tarot decks such as the Tarot de Marseilles (The Deck of

Tarot de Marseilles is an authentic reproduction of Marseilles' famous Tarot)? The centuries-old Tarot was revived by French scholars with crisp illustrations, based on original woodcut pictures., the Visconti Tarot, or the Original Waite Tarot deck? And are you drawn to the conventional (and sometimes independent) Tarot Decks like the Wild Unknown, Fountain Tarot, and Star-child Tarot? I LOVE the latest new Tarot decks now. The artwork is fascinating, and the imagery is essential to modern times. (When did you see a Knight walking the streets last time?!) Well, I love them so much that I made my own!

You can Check out the Helping Book with the Decks

Most Tarot decks are to provide with a book describing the meanings of the artwork and the Tarot card. Some decks do have more details than others, however. And some maybe don't have any details! If you want to know what a card means and why to check out the Little White Book with the Deck to see if it gives you what you need. And, if the book that accompanies you is not enough, search online and see if there is a blog or an eBook that describes the cards in greater detail. On the other hand, you may be pleased to explore and interpret the Tarot cards through your intuition and emotional link, so having no book might just be a blessing!

You can Find a Size that Fits Best

Several Tarot cards come in various sizes. You have to pick which size is right for you. For group Tarot readings or parties, Giant Tarot cards can be perfect. Standard tarot cards may be ideal for face-to-face readings of clients or personal readings. And the mini tarot cards are great for a Tarot reading on the go to fit in your handbag. It is particularly essential for the handling and shuffling of cards. Whether the cards are too big or too small, they may be too cumbersome to manage for you or your customers. So, treat the chips, and practice shuffling them before picking a deck.

You should Consider How to Use the Tarot Cards

Think about what sorts of Tarot readings you want to do and how you want your Tarot cards to interact. Are you trying to find happiness and tranquility in your life? Then the Zen Tarot Osho may be the right Deck for you. Do you need to appeal to your inner goddess? Find the cards of the Mythical Goddess Tarot or the Goddess Tarot instead. Will you have a passion for earthly customs and practices? Then check out the Tarot Deck on Druid Art. The fantastic thing is that from so many different perspectives there are so many Tarot cards, you will find a deck that is ideal for your personal needs and wishes. So if you're a qualified Tarot reader, consider keeping several different Tarot decks on hand, depending on what's energetically best suited for your client so circumstance.

You Should Check the Quality

Some Tarot cards must be of sufficient thickness to ensure you will continue to use them for years to come. However, some poorer reproductions may occur that are not of good quality, and the cardboard can quickly break or become even more rapidly damaged. Best to avoid these cheaper forms, if you intend to use the Tarot cards regularly.

You should not be Afraid to Buy your Tarot Cards

There is a legend that you will only collect Tarot cards and that you cannot buy your own. Okay, what a phooey! I'd like to buy a Tarot deck that I know is a good match, rather than waiting for someone to give me a deck that could just be absolute 'wrong.' And don't worry about buying your Tarot box, instead of waiting for someone to give you one.

2.3 Preparing for Tarot Reading

Now you have your Tarot deck, you've worked out how to keep it free from negativity, and now you're ready for someone else to learn. Maybe it's a friend he's learned about your interest in Tarot. Perhaps it is a sister in need of help from the Coven. Maybe

– and this happens a lot – it's a friend of a friend who has an issue and would like to see "what the future holds." However, there are a few things you can do before you take on another person's duty to read cards. Make sure to read this in advance of reading!

As now you are familiar that the reading of tarot cards is an art that helps you visualize the future. Tarot readings are fascinating whether you are a believer or not, and should never be regarded as gospel truth. You should also not take the cards too literally either; they are here to give you a direction, to guide you on your journey. If you're interested in reading, you need to learn some stuff before you sit down for reading. You need to remember that the tarot readings may be disturbing and can make you anxious about the future. The readings don't need to be pessimistic; you need to take it positively and hope it will make your life even better. Whatever the cards may say, realize that it's not a definite look to your life, it's only leading you toward improving your experience.

A reader of tarot cards will always inspire you to do your best in all aspects of your life. A death card, for instance, doesn't mean you stop living and embrace death as your destiny. It's unavoidable, but you have to believe in yourself and do the best you can in every way. Tarot reading isn't a way to embrace destiny, but it does help you change your life and make better choices. A lot of people don't understand this and have difficulty depending on their reading accuracy.

Have a List of Questions

Getting a list of questions to read beforehand also helps. Offer it some time, and consider what answers you want. When you sit across the tarot reader, questions can become daunting to you. Then bring your thoughts together and make a list of all the items to which you would like answers. Once you're focused about the type of questions you have, the session will be much more successful, and you'll be able to make better use of the time.

Have an Open Mind

It's always easier to predict the unexpected at a tarot reading. Prepare for the unexpected. All is about the energy that flows in and out of the people around you. The tarot reader will tell you plenty of things you may not be prepared for. Logically take this extra material, and do not allow it to distract you. Be mindful that you are now getting ready for your future.

Accept the Energy Inflow

By the end of a tarot reading, most people feel energized. It's the perfect way of elevating morale and being positive about the future. You have to be conscious of the energy that comes in and let it flow into your mind and body. When you're driven in the right direction by the tarot reader, you'll feel good at the end. You'll enjoy the cycle and feel uplifted along the way.

You Do Not Need to Expect Total Accuracy

No astrology can give you an accurate reading of 100 per cent. There is no sure formula for the shot that can convincingly think about the future. Tarot reading is an art that includes analyzing the faces and their meanings, so if you have to hear something you're not prepared for, don't feel bad, you will still be able to accomplish your goals even though the card says you're not going to.

Trust the Reader

You cannot trust their reading unless you have full confidence in the reader. You need to trust the reader before you start a session and be ready to get the best out of it. The course is far more than asking questions and answering them. It's about Recovery and Power. You need to be frank with the reader for this and express your thoughts. You need to unwind and think about your problems freely. Take all that off your chest to find the right direction. Human beings are fascinated with the future. Each of us is only waiting to learn what is going to happen to our lives, desires and goals. Tarot reading is an art that does not provide you with a definitive answer to your questions but may lead you in the right direction and the proper manner.

2.4 The Layout of the Cards

Several spreads, or drawings, may be used to read Tarot cards. Try one of these – or try any of them! –To see the most reliable approach for you. Make sure you begin by reading how to prepare for your reading-it will make things much easier for you! The spreads in this topic are listed in order from the easiest to the most complicated-if you've never read before, start with a basic three-card layout at the top, for yourself or someone else, and work your way down the list. When you become acquainted with the cards and their meanings, trying out more complex formats will become much more straightforward. You can also find that, with one distributed over the others, you get more reliable results. That's a lot happening but don't be frightened.

1. Basic Three Card Layout

If you're a Tarot beginner, the three-card spread is a great place to start learning and have some Tarot card read practice! Even if you're a seasoned Tarot reader, this spread is perfect for getting back to the basics and easy answers. The distribution of the three cards is perfect for indicating some kind of linear direction or sequence of events. The distribution of three cards can be extended to several different questions and circumstances. We will concentrate on the three-card spread for the purpose of this guide, which provides insight into the history, present and future.

For any card reading, first of all, you need to select a sacred space for the reading, then you choose your decks and focus on the intention.

Shuffling the cards can sound easy, but sometimes this move can be challenging. Tarot cards are much larger than playing regular cards, and you'll want to stop bending them. There are different ways to stack your deck, and it's up to you to pick which one you'd like. Here are a few suggestions:

Cut the deck

Split the deck into several separate piles, then bring them back together

Scrambling method

Scatter all the cards on a table or floor, then scramble them together

Inserting method

keep half the deck in each hand. Next, haphazardly drop one part of the deck into the other part.

Now you need to divide your shuffled cards into three separate layouts and then flip over your cards. Flip the top card from left to right onto each mini stack. Then examine your cards. The first card tells the history, the second card explains the present and the third card represents the future means the direction in which you are moving.

The Seven Card Horseshoe Spread

When you improve your Tarot reading skills, you may find you tend to spread one specific over the others. The Seven Card Horseshoe spread is among the most common spreads in use today. Even though it uses seven different cards, it is, in reality, a relatively straightforward set. That card is arranged in such a way that it relates to various aspects of the issue or situation. In this variant of the Seven Card Horseshoe set, in order, the cards reflect the past, the present, secret causes, the querent, attitudes of others, what the querent will do about the situation and the likely outcome.

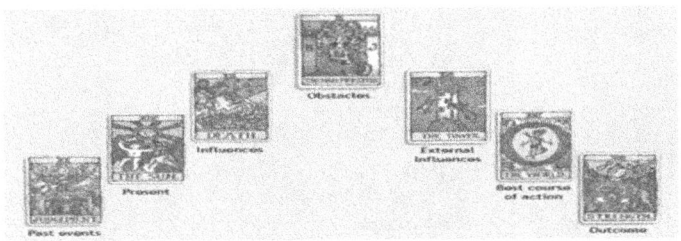

The Pentagram Spread

The next spread of cards uses five cards and provides a little more detail about the question while also indicating the consequence if the querent decides to take a course of action. The cards form a cross inside this set. The center-right card reflects future outcomes. The center card reflects the current situation. The card to the center's left shows history, which still affects the current situation. The card at the bottom represents the reasons which lead to the current situation or cause. The top card represents potential outcomes that can arise while the querent is pursuing an action path. The distribution is most helpful in assisting the questioner decide what to do with a situation.

The Romany Tarot

The spread of the Romany Tarot is natural, but it reveals a surprising amount of detail. It is an excellent spread to use if you are only looking for a general summary of a situation, or when you have several overlapping problems that you are trying to address. It is a relatively free-form spread which leaves plenty of space in your interpretations for flexibility. Many people view the Romany spread as being past, present and future, using the cards in each of the three rows together. In Row A, the more distant history is indicated; the second row of seven, Row B, shows problems currently existing with the querent. The bottom row, Row C, uses seven more cards to explain what is likely to happen in the life of the person if everything continues along the current course. Reading the Romany spread by merely looking at the past, the present and the future is simple. Moreover, if you break it down into its various facets, you will go into greater detail and get a more nuanced view of the situation.

Celtic Cross Spread

The spread of the Celtic cross is the most well-documented distribution of the tarot. It uses ten cards, and the form of a circle and line. This format has been modified and configured by many readers and thus has many variations. A typical spread places a spread of five cards – with one card in the middle, the second card in the top, turned to the side to form a +, three above 1, 4 below 1, 5 on the right and six on the left. Cards 7 through 10 are laid in a line to the side, with card seven at the bottom, and card ten at the top. Each card turns to a slight angle.

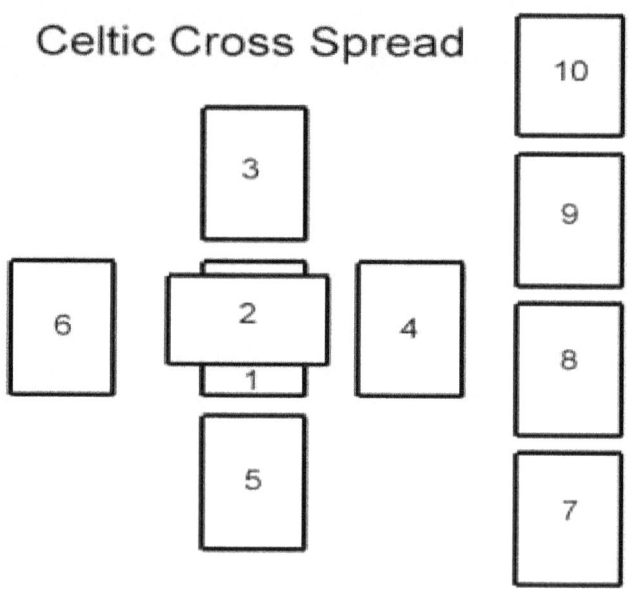

Card one reflects the current state. Card two reflects the existing barriers or troubles. Card three indicates the best result possible. Card four demonstrates the explanation for your present condition. Card Five is your immediate past, and card Six is your immediate future. Card seven reflects who you are in general right now, and how you respond to the subject of the issue. Card eight indicates your current surroundings relevant to your query in terms of family, friends and the environment. Card nine reflects your hopes and concerns about the issue, or at this point in your life in general, if you haven't had a particular question. Card 10 is the product of the query, or else how this stage of your life will turn out.

Tarot readers use the Celtic Cross Tarot Spread as one of the most widely used spreads. But did you know that accurate interpretation is one of the hardest Tarot spreads, too? And while the Celtic Cross spread is in almost every Tarot book and is used by beginners at Tarot, many Tarot readers lack the deeper insights found in this nuanced spread. Yeah, you can read every Tarot card, spread one by one, in the Celtic Cross, but if you want like the Tarot reader everyone talks about, you'll have to master the interactions between the cards and capture the story in your Tarot reading. And here, I'm not only going to show you the Celtic Cross's structure and positions, but I'm also going to teach you exactly how to interpret the Celtic Cross by digging deep into the most critical relationships shared between the cards in the Celtic Cross.

First Card: The Present

This card reflects what happens to the querent. It also reflects the state of mind of the querier and how they may perceive the situation.

Second Card: The Challenge

This card is the immediate challenge or problem the querent faces. It is the one thing which will make life much easier if resolved. Even if in this position you draw a 'good' card, weigh it carefully, because it will always be a challenge.

Third Card: The Past

This card represents the events leading up to the present situation and may give some indication of how the challenge came to pass.

Fourth Card: The Future

This card represents what is likely to happen in the coming weeks or even months. It is not the end goal, merely the next step on the path.

Fifth Card: Above

This card represents the intent, expectation or best outcome of the querent concerning the situation. It is what the querent is actively working towards as they attempt to solve the problem.

Sixth Card: Below

This card reflects what is within the querent's subconscious realm and delves far deeper into the core basis of the situation. It symbolizes the underlying emotions and patterns associated with the case and may show what drives the querent. This card may carry a surprise message to the querent, particularly if they are not deeply connected to their inner being (beware of reversed cards here that are likely to mean that the querent is 'unknown').

Seventh Card: Advice

The advice card takes into consideration all that happens within the life of the querent and offers a suggestion about what action should be taken to tackle the current challenges.

Eight Card: External Influences

This card shows the entities, energies or events that will influence the question's outcome and are beyond the control of the querent.

Ninth Card: Hopes and Fears

That could be one of the toughest positions to understand. Bear in mind that hopes and fears are closely linked, and what we hope for may also be what we are afraid of, and so may fail. Often drawing a second card for clarity after reading is set out and reading the two together is useful.

Tenth Card: Outcome

This card represents where the situation is going, and if/how the question can be solved. It assumes the consequence of following their current course of action, based on the querent. Of course, if the result card isn't a good outcome, it is within the querent's free will to make the required adjustments to their situation.

Astrological Spreads:

The astrological tarot spread uses 12 cards, putting one card like a clock in each location around the circle. This layout is designed to provide a summary of the next 12 months. The first month is the present month, or, if you're close to the end of the month, the next month maybe month one. You can place an optional 13th card in the center of the circle to represent the tone for the entire year. Because a tarot deck has 78 cards, you can create the circle six complete times, with six cards in the center. The more times you move around the globe; the more details you'll get.

Each card represents one of the astrological houses, as follows:

- The self – how others see Problem
- Financial values-property, possessions, and power to earn
- Travel and correspondence-daily
- Home Life-siblings, family, parents
- Pleasure-passion, love, holidays, imagination, expression of oneself

- Job and wellbeing-both physical and mental
- Marriage and partnerships – personal and professional, legal matters
- Starts and ends-conception, death, sex, money from other people, inheritance
- Philosophy, schooling, visions
- Long-distance journeys. Career-fame, fame
- Wishes, friends, hopes
- Burdens – constraints, perils, subconscious, secret fears.

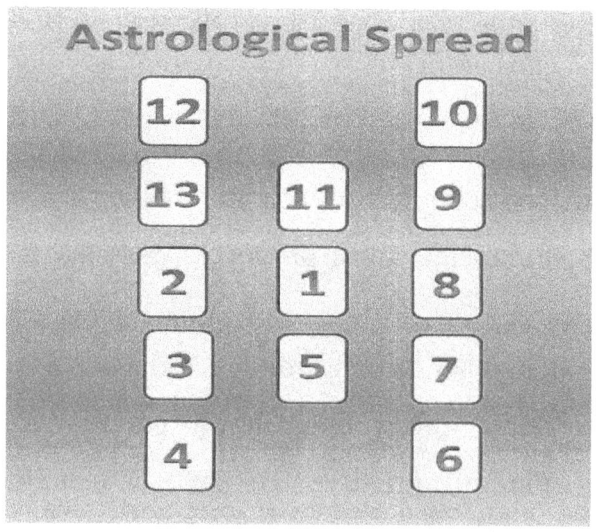

The Success Spread

The success spread an outstanding array of the situation to use when you are facing an obstacle or difficulty, and you don't know how to tackle it and resolve it. This tarot spread helps you understand better the true essence of the challenge that you face. It will help you recognize which skills and tools you have not only to meet in your company but to conquer any obstacles life throws into your own company!

- 1 – The first card reflects the greatest worry or challenge. Who is it you are facing? If you are not exactly sure what it is you can't solve a question, and that's what this card can tell you.
- 2 – The second card outlines the obstacles and problems you face in the current situation. Why does the issue turn up in your life? How does that shape your life course?
- 3 – The third card shows the secret factors which affect your current condition. You need to learn what those variables are to conquer the challenge that you face.

- 4 – The fourth card reflects new ideas, new people or items that could help you to evolve. Through becoming interested in these different ways, the understanding of the situation will change, and you will find better solutions to your problems.
- 5 – The final card indicates what to do to be successful, or what to stay away from to avoid failure. When it is a positive card, it will point you in the direction you need to follow or advise you to stay away from the circumstances indicated when it is a negative card.

Spiritual Spread

Compared to the tarot spread of prosperity, the spread of Spiritual Guidance is used situationally at periods when you encounter spiritual obstacles or challenges. Such barriers are usually related to your spiritual growth or creation. This tarot spread aims to give you a broader perspective and includes information to assist you in your spiritual path and the valuable lessons you will learn about it.

- 1 – The first card reflects your primary concern about your spiritual path, problem or issue. Also, if you may think you know what the problem is, this card shows the true nature of the problem.
- 2 – The second card interprets your inspiration to help you on your journey. Were you motivated by personal benefit, the need for recognition or a position of genuine, humble knowledge that you can improve?
- 3 – The third card describes the things you feel nervous or disheartened about in your

life. What are your perceived flaws, and how do they affect the situation?

- 4 – The fourth card shows the things you are unaware of in your current state. It is typically an external factor or circumstance which directly affects your current state.
- 5-The advice card is the fifth one. It will give you knowledge of what you should or should not be doing to resolve your apprehensions. When you're looking for advice from a real place, this card will tie in with both the second and third cards.
- 6 – The sixth card will tell you the best way to proceed with your thoughts, and what you can do to begin your spiritual journey. We all have our directions to pursue. At this moment, this card is being catered to match your unique needs.
- 7 – The seventh card shows you how to take the positive light forward. Now you can do the new situation to the best of it.
- Notice, If the sixth or seventh card (or both) is negative, you'll either have to fix what's

represented inside yourself or someone or a life circumstance.

- 8 – Eventually, the eighth card wraps up the potential outcome you'll get if you can effectively obey the guiding light shown on the fifth card. Note, as, with all spreading of tarot readings, the result will change depending on how you react to the reading. For example, if the sixth or seventh card is negative, while the eighth card is positive, you would need to work especially hard on the negative factors to obtain a positive outcome. If the sixth or seventh card and the eighth card are negative, the things shown in card six or seven will need to be changed. If both the sixth and seventh cards are positive but the eighth card is a negative look for guidance to the second and third cards. There is also lovespread and relationship spreads.

2.5 Reading Tarot for Yourself

There are hundreds of tarot spreads to choose from, beginning with the basic spread of 3 cards and progressing to the intricate Celtic Cross. Stick to a format that's consistent with your question, and you know it by heart. If you're still not familiar with each role, it won't do you any good to opt for an elaborate spread; likewise, an excessively simplistic spread will provide little insight into a more complicated matter. Those who practice the Tarot or deal on their spiritual creation sometimes wonder if they can read Tarot. The general issue appears to be that it is possible to be impartial when it's a reading for you as opposed to whether you might give someone else a psychic reading. The short answer is, yes you can read Tarot for yourself! Because of their incredible symbolism, I genuinely love Tarot cards, but you'll hear me say again and again that they are the core of our purpose and capability. The magic is in us, not them, and that magic is the intuitive wisdom we all have to help direct us through life. That's why you are allowed to read for yourself. So. the problem that we have to start with is, how are you tuned to your intuitive instincts before you pick up the cards and start using them?

Psychic development means practicing tuning in to our instincts and paying attention to it as a source of insight just as important as something you may see or hear. It can also be more relevant as we can interpret and listen to what we see, while our perception is generally straightforward. One actually may not be paying attention to it, because it is not respected in our 'rational' culture. After all, we drown it out with the noise of daily life. It may be because it goes against what we want to be the case; we may dull our ability to tap into our psychic intuition.

The way to make yourself better at reading is this. Start holding a journal, and as you read for yourself, reveal ultimately everything that springs to your mind without wondering or censoring yourself for a second time. Only put all of that on paper. You must get used to knowing that something that comes in is coming from your own intuitive experience and when your voice starts to fade in. Besides, make a note of how you felt when you did the reading. Were you relaxed and open-minded? Were you anxious, frustrated, or finding it hard to focus otherwise? What did you feel at the reading of what you saw?

You will be able to look back over time and objectively calculate how close you were to what you wrote down by the way things happen. The clear feedback will allow you to see where you are doing well and where you may need to get better. What you'll probably notice is that you're more open to respond to what your intuition is trying to tell you when you're relaxed and receptive, and as a result, you're doing a better reading. So, before you pick up the cards, you can start playing with how to construct a strong and centered feeling. With this, daily meditation does help. Just do it and look at what happens for a few weeks!

Avoid these Common Mistakes during Reading

Reading during a Highly Emotional Time:

If it's rage or anxiety or pain in the immediate aftermath of a moment, we're never in the right mental state to think with composure and clarity. As after a difficult fight with a friend or break-up with an ex you might want to dive for the chips, try resisting. Take at least a few days to let the metaphoric dust settle down and bring your thoughts together. Intense and urgent emotions rarely make readings enlightening, and the cards will probably represent nothing more than your inner turmoil. Taking some time off the upset to relax, pause, and recover. Meditate on what you mean by the case, and what you want to know from it. You can find that after all, a particular event that at the moment seemed harrowing is of no real harm, or the break-up was what you wanted and are now thankful for.

Repeating a Spread for the Same Questing for Multiple Times

Once it comes to a tarot reading, let's face it, we don't always get the answers we would like. Reshuffling, asking again, and interpreting a new spread in the privacy of a personal reading is an instinct for newly acquainted tarot readers. Do try to avoid giving yourself several readings on the same question, however understandable, in hopes of a different response. For each new reading, this will just further muddle the cards and their meanings.

Drawing Extra Cards

You might also be tempted to pull "clarifier" cards instead of repeating a spread in believe of getting additional information or, better yet, answers that are positive to your desired outcome. For example, if you're going to get the dream job you've applied for, you want to know, but the cards show something less-than-promising prospect – so you'll draw a couple more, looking for a silver lining. Seek to abstain from doing so as with numerous spreads. Reflect on the initial spread in hand and seek to view the messages of the cards with a free and objective mind.

Finding a Meaning According to Your Desire

A common criticism about tarot reading is that each card's ultimate meaning rests with the reader. Innumerable guides and forums and books are there to tell you what every card and model means. The problem is they contradict almost everyone! A reading of a tarot card requires intuition and the capacity to see beyond one's instilled desires, prejudices and anxieties. When you are looking at a personal spread that gives rise to anxiety or frustration, explore that rather than rushing to your computer to look up alternate definitions. ('Hey, maybe the Death Card means THIS instead of THAT ...') You'll intensify your uncertainty and self-doubt if you continue to second-guess what you intuitively know to be real, even though that reality is disturbing.

Tarot Reading for Others

You may want to give your loved ones, relatives, acquaintances, colleagues at work or strangers to read cards. Some may even actively try you to read a Tarot to them. Everyone has their Tarot viewpoint and opinions, based on an endless amount of tools, and people have several different preconceptions and different perceptions of how and what Tarot can bring. It's essential to explain what your Tarot views are and how you use it for people so they can determine if your reading style fits their needs. Some people love the Tarot and have a strong understanding of it, but never feel customers confident reading. Every reader has to decide that, but I've always loved to read for others. It's important to note that it's a privilege to help others and it should be taken even as you enjoy reading and interacting with your clients. Before starting to read professionally, I think every reader should have a code of ethics; it will make both you and the questioner more relaxed, or querent.

Here Are Some Helpful Tips When You Do Tarot Reading for Others

When a reader wants to communicate with the spirit to guide someone else, a short blessing often sets the mood before reading. Everything you want, you should tell. One example is, "I devote this deck to serving others with spiritual development, awareness, and bringing peace to all who seek their wisdom. My favorite is anyone who uses and touches this deck realizes the love of spirit. They find their spirit of light inside.

It's not uncommon for a mother to turn over a tarot deck to her daughter or son, and to save the deck from mom for family and close friends readings. My mum brought me my first deck of Tarot. The vibrations of other people come through the panels, and I want to save that one for my most intimate readings and provide another for readings of the clients.

Many people have difficulty getting tarot cards shuffled. It needs quite a bit of practice. New decks are better since at first, the cards are slippery.

However happy they are, the client can mix them; there's no right or wrong way to go. If it helps, they can spread them all out as "Go Fish" game for a child. Only make sure to get the cards shuffled adequately. If you start turning the cards and get two or three in your last reading, return them to the customer for more shuffling. Also, if you start turning cards and they don't make sense about the problem or don't feel right, stop and re-shuffle. It is what is considered a "garbage reading." While the Tarot has a sense of humor and often addresses a question that has not been asked, when it happens, you will know one of these readings. Start on.

When the customer puts the cards back together for reading, the cards should be split into three piles and then placed together in the order of their choosing before returning them to the reader.

Lie down the cards, so that the reader can face you. Not quite the other way around.

How to store the tarot cards? Some prefer wrapping them in a piece of silk or holding them in a pouch of silk. A beautiful looking wooden box is also the right way of protecting them.

You need to "clean" the deck between readings, not necessarily every time, but relatively frequently, as the vibrations of other people get in the cards. You can clear them by merely scanning each card, placing the cards in a sunny window for a while. You can clean them by placing on top of the deck a cleaning crystal of your choosing. Amethyst and smoky quartz are two beautiful crystals that cleanse. We will discuss the cleaning of cards in details in the next topic.

I find it best to have two decks when reading out of work or if you have numerous people who come to your home for reading. I like seeing one of the Main Arcana cards broken off from the other. Some of the readings I prefer using just certain cards, and I don't like splitting them between customers anyway.

You should make readings yourself. Just do it, and make sure you've determined what card positions mean and where they're going before you try it out on someone else!

It's also essential to set proper moods. Light a scented candle, and have a lovely piece of cloth set for the cards drawn for reading. Softly played in the background, a calming CD is always good too. Try to read in a position as quiet as you can, so you can focus.

2.6 How to Clean Tarot Decks?

There is a tradition of purifying and clearing new, and old, tarot cards in the tarot culture.

Here's the good news: It's both optional and straightforward.

Many readers may not wipe their tarot decks – which is utterly perfect. I know those who don't clean their cards, and the readers are great. But many people do believe their tarot cards are capable of having energetic gunk stuck on them. And why would you like to clean your tarot cards, or bless them?

If they are used- Who knows who owned the deck. Is there an obsessive, nervous or derogatory energy surrounding their use? As the new owner, it's best to freshen them up and get them tuned to you.

When they were struck by someone else – this is a piece of polarizing tarot legend. Some practitioners of tarot will not let anyone touch their cards.

Given what your tarot teacher insisted, or what you read in a manuscript, it's optional to stick to that belief.

When you find that after someone touches them your cards read differently, then don't let the folks contact them. It's a personal preference otherwise – not a hard-fast statute. Do good tarot etiquette practice: inquire first, before touching the tarot deck of another person.

When your readings are regularly negative or ambiguous – there could be odd electrical gunk attached to your cards that will muck the reading. Reading on a negative situation will yield negative card results. But occasionally you get a weird, inexplicably unpleasant vibe that needs explanation.

Too much reading on a subject will cause the readings to become confused. The common practice then is to let the deck "rest" or restart by sweeping it up.

You feel the need to reconnect with a deck – cleaning or clearing them is a perfect way to reconnect if your cards have been put away for a while. The same applies to an older deck you plan to use again.

1. Incense/Smudging

One of the most common methods by which tarot cards are cleaned is by incense.

In rites of purification, many religious practices burn incense. Throughout the West, white sage, sweet grass, or Palo Santo are the most common incenses used for cleansing. Palo Santo is my favorite with a woody and light flavor.

You can use a stick, cone, or loose incense, too. Use an incense that has related properties for blessing or cleansing.

Many readers clean every card, one at a time, in their deck. So if you want the entire deck to have a go at it, do that.

Cleaning yourself or your reading room is also a good idea to flush out any tension around you. Smudging yourself with tarot readers before and after readings (especially when reading for someone else) is a common practice.

Whether you like incense but have awful allergies and smoke addiction, use sprays made from essential oils instead—spray to clean up work thoroughly.

Sprays can be used in several base oils -sage, Palo Santo, etc. For that aura-cleansing-goodness to work, spritz your room and yourself. Be careful not to spray your cards deliberately, or risk damaging them. Smudging is a collective term for the cleaning of incense.

2. Under the Full Moon

Put your tarot decks in a window sill, or on a table where they are struck by full moonlight. Each 29-ish days the Moon is full. You can get applications that alert you to the full Moon a few days before. I use Astro Rx calendar from Deluxe Moon Pro and Briana Saussy which can be exported to your computer. When the moon switches phase it passes even around the zodiac wheel's twelve locations. If you want the energy to be intensified, you can also use the full moon zodiac sign to fill your deck with purpose.

Capricorn, for example, has an attraction to industry, profession and authority. Let's assume in Capricorn; for instance, it is a full moon. Under that Moon, you could clean and charge your deck to imbue it with business- and career-related assets. That night, or the next day, you might read for yourself or clients on business or career-related matters. Your deck will have a little extra oomph on Capricorn-ruled subject matters. But if that's too difficult, then plain old moonlight is still working fine!

3. A Sun Bath

Unlike a moon bath, on a rainy day, or at a spot where they will obtain enough sunshine, you should leave your cards off. I wouldn't suggest this if you're living in a humid climate-unless you're bothered by twisted or bent cards. I had cards warping from late-afternoon sun exposure, even on my reading table indoors. Granted, I'm living in a dry, humid area. Your mileage could change! Also, this is a perfect system to use if you want to charge good, radiant energy on your cards.

4. Singing Bowl

If you've got one, then try. Many folks claim the bowls' sound will cleanse people or artifacts and attune them. Place your deck in the bowl as you ring it, or in the presence of the bowl.

5. Reiki

Reiki is a calming energy device using energy channeled through the hands. Practitioners are usually accredited by an instructor or organization within the program. Try this as a way to clean your cards, if you know Reiki. If in Reiki, you are not trained, try meditating with intent while holding the cards in your hands.

6. Salt

Most readers swear by the process of salting. Wrap your cards in plastic and cover the deck within a salt jar. If the idea resonates with you, then try. Personally, it looks too messy, along with risking card loss (can you tell me how picky I am with my cards yet?). But, again, the approach is valued by many tarot practitioners.

Here's a less messy suggestion: put your cards on top of a salt slab of the Himalayas. These can be found in most major grocery stores.

7. Crystals

One of the most common forms of cleaning and cleansing a Tarot deck is through crystal potent strength. By selecting one or more crystals which absorb negative energy, you can easily clean and recharge your Tarot Deck. Place on top of the deck a piece of Selenite, Black Tourmaline or Amethyst and leave it to do its thing. If you choose

Transparent Quartz to do the job, the strength of the Tarot cards is also enhanced.

8. Knocking on the Deck

That's Okay. Knock on your tarot deck three times, just as you'd do a door.

I had it clarified to me that the cards are both transparent and "wakes up" my inner animist is fond of that notion. It is probably the best and purest form to use in pinch clearing.

9. Blowing on the Cards

Some readers clear their cards by fanning and blowing the deck out. Cleaning up your breath is an exciting process. I don't know the origin of this practice, but it reminds me of folklore gambling. There's a tradition in the Baccarat card game where players blow to the cards to take away bad luck. In dice-based games, where players blow on dice for good luck, you can see this custom too. Perhaps this is a continuing tradition from the early history of tarot as a game of cards. For a lot of people, it works anyway!

10. Visualization or Meditation

The methods of visualization or meditation work well for cleaning tarot cards. Imagine a ball of light that cleans the cards or wind that sweeps away the leftover energy. That can be done as you shuffle or keep the deck in your hands. Similarly, some writers recite prayers to cleanse their cards and charge them. Tell yourself what you want your deck to support you with while creating a meditation or prayer for your cards. Some examples include encouragement from your spirit or higher self, helping your clients, assisting with healing or shadow work, etc.

11. Reordering the Deck and Shuffling

It is one of my favorite ways of getting acquainted with a deck that has been in storage for some time or finding a new deck. To do this, first reorder a shuffled deck with Arcana Major, followed by Arcana Minor. So for me, I start at 0 with the Fool and last at 22 with the World. Instead, I stack the Ace-10 suits with the court cards in order from Title, Knight, Queen to King. I put all of them back in a stack (no choice what suit comes first with). It is similar to pressing the reset button on a tarot deck for me. It even refreshes my memory on deck images I haven't seen in a while. Occasionally new insights into a card's oimagery can pop up in this process. Each of the above strategies can be mixed and combined. Test one out and see if the readings work. Hopefully, you have found a form of cleaning that is resonating with you. If not, make no worries! There are also brilliant, talented writers who don't use any of these forms of washing.

Part 3: Interpretation of Tarot Cards and their Meaning

The phenomenon is called synchronicity, a concept invented by psychologist Carl Jung to explain the occurrence of events that coincide temporally. There is no difference, in synchronicity, between inner and outer. The choice of a card is precisely what you already know about your higher self. The dialogue with your higher self is what tarot occultists call it. Sometimes the cards do work. It's not magic — the tarot cards are a sacred mirror.

Types of Decks

Hundreds of types of tarot decks are now available to choose from, Hello Kitty to Zombies. A typical deck has 22 Arcana Major (or trumps) that are the archetypal pictures. There are 56 cards for Minor Arcana, 16 cards for Court or Personality; the Kings, Queens, Princes and Pages, much like modern cards for play. Four components or suits exist Fire, Earth, Air and Water, each with ten cards in. Some cards are necessarily negative.

There's a lot of ways to work with the deck. You will pick your deck by intuitively being drawn to it. Including Kabbalah, the tree of life, color scales, Hebrew symbols, numerology, patterns, symbolism, alchemy, astrology, mythology and learning to meditate directly with each card are layers on layers of structures to understand. The further levels you gain information and insight into the cards

Check out what each Tarot card means, including the keywords, meaning, and card stories. Those are my Tarot card interpretations I use in my Tarot readings every day-and now you can use them as well! Let specific meanings of the Tarot card be your guide, not your faith. The Tarot cards don't have 'right' or 'wrong' meanings. There are, of course, conventional definitions of what the Tarot cards mean, but I encourage you to believe your instincts and go along with the meanings that sound right for you.

3.1 The Major Arcana

The most identifiable and impactful cards in a Tarot deck are the Major Arcana ones. Such 22 cards reflect challenges that we all face in the grand life scheme, each bearing unique messages of wisdom and advice to assist you in times of necessity. These Major Arcana cards show clues about your life's bigger picture and its long-term direction. Although each of the Major Arcana cards stands alone with their deep meanings and influences, these 22 Tarot cards tell a story too. The first card, The Fool, is the principal character of this story, and the 21 cards that follow reflect his experiences as he learns, develops and makes his way through life. This plot is a perfect summary of the successes, failures, and lessons we all experience as we go through the trials and troubles of our lives, growing up to the end of our journey into pure, full Beings.

Zero: The Fool

The first card in a Tarot deck is the Fool because he is the weakest of all the archetypes of the Tarot. He has not yet witnessed the ups and downs of life, leaving him unaware of the extent of the complexities of life and the power and potential that he carries. When The Fool shows up in a Tarot reading, you're encouraged to take on his free, willing energy and accept without worry all that lies ahead of you.

Magician

The Magician card reminds you that you are a particular person and have a lot of talents most people don't have. Those skills distance you from the crowd and can help you launch new projects or resolve adversity. When The Magician comes up reading your Tarot, it's a reminder you don't have to wait — you're already keeping everything you need to move forward and accomplish what you've set out to do.

The High Priestess

A card of knowledge and sub consciousness is the most intuitive, linked card in the entire Tarot deck, The High Priestess. This card supports listening to your inner voice and trusting your intuition. Your mind knows much, far more than you think, and The High Priestess embodies this idea. Avoid searching for answers in the outside world when she appears in your Tarot reading and then turns in for the direction you are searching for.

The Empress

The Empress is a Major Arcana, or "trump" coin, which depicts the grandmother's strength. She is nature, the ever-unfolding source of life-giving power, around us but also inside us. The Empress is also portrayed as a pre-Christian Goddess. It is like the one channeling The High Priestess down to Earth for the majority of us. Empress Card was painted in medieval Europe to represent whatever queen ruled the land at present, possibly to appease the Inquisitors. Yet the scholars of the Renaissance and beyond had no question about her true identity — until after the French Revolution, she could not be wholly identified on Tarot cards as "the woman clothed with the light" The ultimate femininity archetype even symbolizes fertility. It is The Empress that gives us nutrition and protection. Sometimes, she is also seen as delighting us with flowers and berries. A potentially frightening dimension of this archetype is embodied each time karmic mood swings wipe out our plans, like a hurricane that has come upon us. The Empress is the root of our nature and moral law, whatever happens. Maybe she could also be named "The Big Recycler."

The Emperor

The Emperor Tarot card represents, in the most realistic words, the highest leadership, a head of state or the most exceptional and influential individual in the world. This archetypal monarch is responsible for the affairs of a society or culture that are directly proportional to his satisfaction and well-being. The more this force brings salvation and spiritual insight; the more comfortable life is for everyone. The archetype of Emperor dominates material nature and physical appearance. When adding this card to your situation, consider your mastery ability. Reinforce a sense of autonomy within you, given any self-limiting values, behaviors or different appearances.

The Hierophant Tarot

This deck, the Hierophant Tarot refers to a master and the learning of practical lessons from natural law analysis. The energy of the card points to some agent or power that can disclose the mysteries of creation, the Moon and tides cycles, the links between humans and the heavens. Since monasteries were the only places in the Middle Ages where a person could learn to read and write, a Hierophant was one to whom a student would apply for admission. It was he who set the framework for the study course of the neophyte. The Hierophant, frequently portrayed with his right hand raised in blessing, is related to the ancient lineage of Melchezidek, the initiator of the Hebrew priestly tradition, the one who passes on the teachings. This archetype is what all shamans of every culture draw upon.

The Lovers

While in some modern decks it has undergone a purely romantic revision of meaning, historically The Lovers Tarot card represented the difficulties of selecting a partner. One cannot take all directions at a crossroads. The photos in various decks on this card have ranged more than others because we've had so many ways to look at sex and relationships through cultures and centuries. Classically, this card's strength reminded us of the real difficulties that romantic relationships face, with the protagonist mostly seen in either-or-choice acting. Sharing a higher goal always necessitates sacrificing the lesser alternative. Eventually, the road of pleasure leads to diversion from spiritual development. Finally, the personality's satisfaction gives way to a call from heaven as the soul matures. Modern decks seem to depict with this card the feeling of romantic love, showing Adam and Eve at Eden's door, when all was still fine. This definition describes society before the crash, and it can be taken to mean a particular kind of option — the option of development over perfection, or the choice of personal growth by friendship rather than a dream where everything falls seamlessly into place and is cared for effortlessly.

The Chariot Tarot

The Chariot Tarot card points to a victorious sense of independence as if a hero (or heroine) is parading the Charioteer through the streets. The card expresses congratulations on good results and acts as a symbol of empowerment. Huge wheels and frisky steeds accelerate the pace at which the force of the driver's will can be achieved. This sort of charge makes the world more available to one brave enough to take the reins of The Chariot. In this feeling of liberation, with an increased pace of change and ability to magnify errors of judgment, there is a risk. The Charioteer is called upon as a seasoned warrior to be extra-attentive to the path ahead.

The Strength Tarot

The Strength Tarot card reflects nature that is tamed by our subtler, more exceptional selves — our feminine hand, our inner selves, however wild it may be in its primitive form. Our intuitive nature's will and passion need not be broken, but perfected, and brought to consciousness so that all aspects of creation can be brought into harmony. The feminine soul-force includes a power of persuasion that can cultivate and encourage cooperation from others by harmonizing differences in the spirit of mutual goodwill.

The Hermit

Check what each Tarot card means, including keywords, definitions, and stories about the deck. Such are my Tarot card interpretations that I use every day in my Tarot readings - and now you can also use them! Let the Tarot card's unique significances be your guide, not your confidence. The Tarot cards have no sense of 'right' or 'wrong.' Of course, there are traditional interpretations of what the Tarot cards mean, but I urge you to trust in your intuition and go along with the meanings that sound right for you.

Wheel of Fortune

The Wheel of Fortune spins continuously sometimes you'll be at the top, and sometimes you'll be at the bottom. This Tarot card tells you that nothing is irreversible and, whether good or bad, you have to enjoy the lessons this moment brings to you. The Wheel of Fortune is one of the deck's highly symbolic cards, loaded with signs, each of which has its significance. A giant circle, lined with abstract symbols, lies at the middle of the card. Numerous creatures surround the wheel, i.e., the angel, the eagle, the bull and the lion. We belong to four-set Zodiac Signs-Leo, Taurus, Scorpio and Aquarius. Those four species are also symbols of Christian practices for the four evangelists, which is perhaps the reason they're all decorated with wings. The books kept by each of the creatures reflect the Torah, which communicates knowledge and understanding of oneself. The snake refers to the act of descent into the material world. A sphinx is riding at the top on the wheel itself. It is with what appears to be either a demon or Anubis himself riding up at the bottom. Such two Egyptian figures are symbolic of both god and king wisdom (in the case of the sphinx) as well as the underworld (Anubis). Both spins in a loop for forever and say that when one comes up, the other goes down.

Upright Wheel of Fortune Love Meaning

Life is riddled with unpredictable changes, and love is no different. The explanation of the Wheel of Fortune tarot love will signify significant changes in your relationship; probably one you did not see coming. These aren't necessarily bad things, but adjustments may have to be made. The relationship you have with your partner will now be checked and you may have to make some effort or compromise to stay together. If you want to make the option, your relationship can get closer than ever as both of you learn to manage the ups and downs of life as a team together. It's necessary to consider whether the changes are positive or negative since the wheel is still spinning.

Upright Wheel of Fortune Career Meaning

There will be many changes when it is about your job. If you are considering making a turn in your career path or role, it may be an excellent time to make those moves now. Try to be more conscious of the possibilities now open to you in your area, to say yes when they arise. Often the changes coming your way may be complicated and daunting, but in fact, these can be blessings for you to improve your skills and prepare you for future development. Embrace those shifts and adapt to them. Going with the flow of these changes will likely bring you success.

Upright Wheel of Fortune Finances Meaning

The Wheel of Fortune often recommends adjustment when it comes to your finances, so be able to adjust to whatever comes your way. If you have been financially secure, make sure to keep putting aside a certain amount to get you through tough times. When you're struggling with material deprivation, be confident that this isn't supposed to last forever. Keep your eyes open to whatever possibilities open up to you.

Justice

This card represents sitting between two pillars, wearing a green robe with two lapels. That individual shown is carrying a two-edge sword in one hand and scales with two pans in the other.

Tarot's Justice represents your soul-self make a destiny decision between two vital choices: Will you continue your life as it is or do you take immediate action to change it? When Justice appears in your life, it means that your soul has adequate. You want true happiness and profound meaning now, but you need to analyze your outer life using inner wisdom to achieve these. You must be honest with yourself and do so as an act of love for yourself.

The Hanged Man

The Hanged Man represents peace of mind in the most basic sense which comes from personal understanding and experience. It's when you know not to make a fuss over small details or changing circumstances, and choose to make delicious lemonade with the hands of lemon life. Although you understand that life cannot always be flawless or to your taste, you too have been wise enough to know that both the good and the bad come and go, and then come and go again. What is left is what you have learned and how much you have evolved. The Hanged Man is such a good omen, a genuinely great card to have on every card spread. It is often shifting the sense of the whole reading. In essence, mainly if it's bad reading, the presence of The Hanged Man means you'll be able to appreciate the unfortunate situation better, remain calm, and act in the best possible way to bring about good results. It's also a great card to imagine, reflect, and meditate on if you are feeling pessimistic, confused, or out of focus. Note how calm the card figure is even when it's upside down. Also, with one leg bent he is so chilling, all the strength and light around his head, symbolizing wisdom and spiritual awakening. If painting is fun for you, you can paint this card too.

The Death Card

The Death card marks the end of the soul's dark night. In the context, the Sun is rising. You've been through a lot, and now, at last, you're entering a time full of love and light. The armored skeleton represents the fossilized customs. Such habits can vary from smoking or eating junk foods to dating abusive people or working in toxic workplaces. Such habits have dominated your life path too long, and now you know that it is time to relegate them from the driver's seat. The black flag's white flower symbolizes innocence and new beginnings. Tarot's Death takes a late start to your soul – your wounds are healed, and you can look forward to a blissful relationship, another work, life-changing decisions, or moving to a special place.

The temperance Card

The Temperance card is a soul-reference. Classically feminine, the woman or angel on the Temperance card mixes up a combination of subtle energies for personality development. You will find one key to reading this card in its title — a play on the method of tempering metals in a forge. Metals must be exposed to extremes of temperature, folding, and pounding, but the final product is vastly superior to unclean earth mined metal.

The Devil

The Devil Tarot card represents the world of the taboo, i.e., the historically rejected wildness and undigested dark side that each of us holds inside our subconscious. This shadow is at the core of our being, which we cannot get rid of and will never succeed in taming. The Devil evoked the church-fueled fear that a person would "lose his soul" to wild and violent powers from his earliest stories, which depicted a vampire-demon.

The Tower Card

Disaster is hitting or has just hit in virtually all Tower Card renditions. The spirits of madness and desperation are set free from ancient hiding places, and nature conspires to destabilize a world with human failures. The chaos is impersonal and mutual. Let's note that these pictures were made for the nobles and clergy who were educated — telling them that if the order is overturned, they have the most to lose. Lightning is an acceptable karmic payback for the culpability of those whose riches come from abusing or abusing others. A modern subtitle might be "revolution" which means that marginalized people will find renewed hope of better times through dramatic social change. The Tower encounter comes as a bolt of lightning to overturn the hegemony of the old order, after which everyone can continue fresh on an equal footing.

The Star Tarot Card

The Star Tarot card is about reconnecting one's soul with the sacred- the transcendent of nature, culture, community and reputation. Ultimately it has to do with the right to be one's self. The soul responds to celestial influences powers which can give a stronger sense of intent to the personality. The Star Card makes us recall our exalted roots and our drive toward a greater community. This card may also be called The Celestial Mandate that which leads us back to our raison d'être, our life mission. The Star tells us that in our daily lives we are, in a way, agents of the divine will. If we let go of the expectation that we should be in charge, we can more readily recognize and appreciate the synchronicities that nudge us along with them. In this way, we are more mindful of the unseen helping hand, and we understand better our position inside and importance to the greater cosmos.

The Moon Card

The Moon card represents to a deep state of sensitivity and creative impressionability which develops within a womb of deep relaxation. Here we dream and go into a trance, have visions and get insights, flow in and out with the spiritual waves and encounter dark magical and frightening experiences beyond our ordinary senses. We can't always regulate what happens in a state of expanded consciousness. The Moon card is the most crucial test of the dignity of a person. In this card, the boundary between the self and the unknown is broken. The loss in identity re-enters the ocean of being. What happens next is between a Creator and a Spirit.

The Sun

The Sun is an uplifting card that reflects happiness, joy, strength and optimism. When The Sun is in your reading of the Tarot, it is a good sign that things go well for you and that you are going in the right direction. Lift your eyes, and remember all the positive things and people around you now and forever.

Judgment

Judgment tells a transformative story, but unlike Death or the Tower, it's not a sudden transformation or born out of luck or chance, but a change that comes out of necessity. It means plans that come to fruition, always long in preparation. When it points to the future, it can also refer to the essence of the change; if you have to make a choice, ruminate and let your mind direct the decision. In this case, logic is a better guide than intuition. Be ready in your life to make a big decision, probably one that will form the next chapter of your life.

The World Card

The World Card marks to the presiding wisdom that upholds life on this planet and every world. It is a female figure in most Tarot decks that have become our traditional World picture. She originates in Hebrew, Gnostic, and Alchemical mythology. She stands between heaven and earth as the celestial mother of souls, God's wife, and our shield from the karmic powers of our immaturity and ignorance that we have set loose upon the earth.

MAJOR ARCANA

FOOL (0)	MAGICIAN (1)	HIGH PRIESTESS (2)	EMPRESS (3)
Beginning Spontaneity Faith Apparent Folly	Action Conscious Awareness Concentration Power	NonAction Unconscious Awareness Potential Mystery	Motherhood Abundance Senses Nature
EMPEROR (4)	HIEROPHANT (5)	LOVERS (6)	CHARIOT (7)
Fatherhood Structure Authority Regulation	Education Belief Systems Conformity Group Identification	Relationship Sexuality Personal Beliefs Values	Victory Will Self-Assertion Hard Control
STRENGTH (8)	HERMIT (9)	WHEEL OF FORTUNE (10)	JUSTICE (11)
Strength Patience Compassion Soft Control	Introspection Searching Guidance Solitude	Destiny Turning Point Movement Personal Vision	Justice Responsibility Decision Cause and Effect
HANGED MAN (12)	DEATH (13)	TEMPERANCE (14)	DEVIL (15)
Letting Go Reversal Suspension Sacrifice	Ending Transition Elimination Inexorable Forces	Temperance Balance Health Combination	Bondage Materialism Ignorance Hopelessness
TOWER (16)	STAR (17)	MOON (18)	SUN (19)
Sudden Change Release Downfall Revelation	Hope Inspiration Generosity Serenity	Fear Illusion Imagination Bewilderment	Enlightenment Greatness Vitality Assurance
	JUDGEMENT (20)	WORLD (21)	
	Judgment Rebirth Inner Calling Absolution	Integration Accomplishment Involvement Fulfillment	

3.2 The Minor Arcana

A series of 56 Minor Arcana Tarot cards following the 22 Main Arcana cards have the power to describe the life of a person based on the symbols represented in those cards, and how they influence different aspects of life. The Major Arcana, also named in a tarot reading as high potential cards, determines the course of the reading. In contrast, the Minor Arcana cards play a supporting role in providing a deeper meaning to the results of the reading. Simply, if the Major Arcana cards are the boldest, most popular colors on your life's canvas, the Minor Arcana cards are the softer shades and tints that play an extraordinarily important role in bringing art and variety to life.

What Does a Minor Arcana Mean in Tarot Reading?

A reading of a Tarot card is based on the cards, taken from the 78 card deck. In a reading, the 56 Minor Arcana tarot cards signify circumstances of everyday life that currently affect your life. These help to give meaning to the reading, as these types of tarot cards reflect the memories, learnings, relationships, thoughts, and feelings you encounter as you begin your life's journey. Whatever situations a person is going through in their lives, they are told by the Minor Arcana cards that this condition is not permanent and will pass, but how it affects you will depend on how you want to behave.

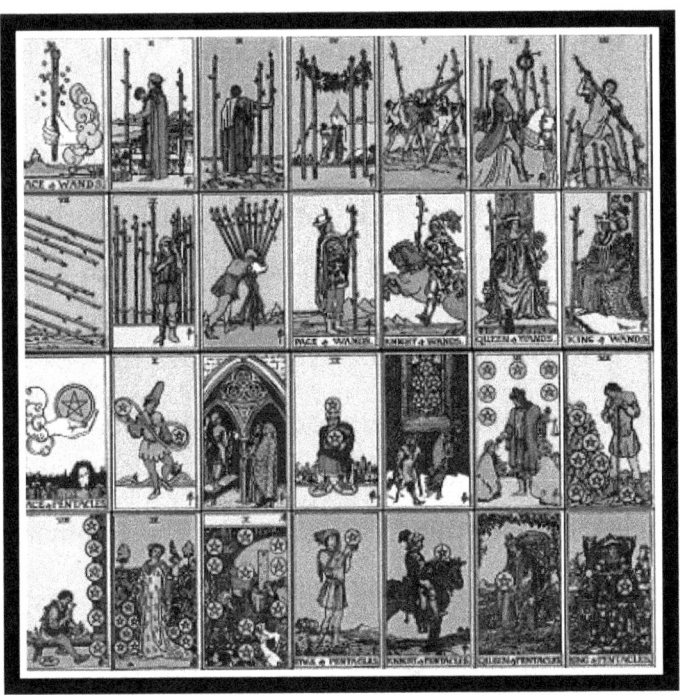

The Minor Arcana Suits and their Meanings

56 Minor Arcana tarot cards offer your lives assurance and meaning through the reading of the tarot cards. These 56 cards are sub-divided into four suits, and each has 14 cards, mirroring the four key elements of life and each Suit reflects various facets of the personality and expressing the part of our lives they affect.

Four Suits of Minor Arcana

The Suit of Cups

The Suit of Cups shows the element 'Water'. This Suit is associated with your thoughts, intuitions, inner feelings and imagination. The Cups also appear in readings that refer to your emotional bond and relationships with others and with you.

The Suit of Pentacles

The Suit of Pentacles reflects Earth's elements. The Suit is connected to the possession of material objects, finances and life at work. The Pentacles also turn up in work and wealth readings.

The Suit of Swords

The Suit of Swords depicts the dimension of Air. Your emotions, expectations, sentences, acts and thoughts are connected with this Suit. The Swords also show up in readings relating to decision-making, communication, and strength and power reinforcement.

The Suit of Wands

The Suit of Wands dimension is Fire, reflecting your spirit, courage, inner-passion and natural inclinations. The Wands cards also appear in readings relating to faith, meaning of life, and beliefs.

List of Minor Arcana Cards from the Suit of Cups

56 Minor tarot Arcana cards are divided into four suits, with 14 cards each. The Suit is numbered with four court cards-The Post, The Knight, The Queen, and The King-from Ace to Ten. These are similar to a play card deck suits with an extra card in each Suit, in a way. While the number of cards of different tarot suits describes and represent various facets of your personality and your current position in life. In general, the court cards represent the people who play a significant role in shaping your life in the present situation. The fundamental element of life is Water which symbolizes human emotions and imagination. Just as life without Water is beyond the boundaries of

possibility, the person can't go forward in any area of existence without the intervention of his feelings, creativity and imagination. Each card in the Suit of Cups illustrates the various levels our emotions influence and control our lives at.

Let's look at the list of Minor Arcana Cards from the Suit of Cups:

Ace of Cups

The tarot card Ace of Cups reflects some of the most significant Minor Arcana beginnings. Those of family and heart. Expanding the heart may involve a spiritual start or a consciousness journey into more excellent experiences.

Two of Cups

The partnership is the single resounding theme synonymous with Two of Cups. What kind of relationship is less straightforward, but you are part of a strong one in the past, present, or future? The relationship must require full trust and command respect. It can be a deeply passionate love affair, of course, but it could just as quickly be a deep and lasting friendship. The exact nature can, or may not, be exposed by the remainder of the set. To you, though, it will be a source of joy, a presence in your life that you can count on at any turn and whose well-being will be as important to you as your own.

Three of Cups

When you draw the Three of Cups, in a celebration of some kind, you can see three women holding their cups high in the Air. Good times are in the Air, for the three ladies have wreaths in their hair made from flowers. Wreaths are also synonymous with achievement and Victory, and they deserve their happiness. The ladies are also seen standing on top of a field of flowers and fruit, adding to the card's happy feelings further. There are feelings of beauty, development, compassion, and happiness which the women share.

Four of Cups

The Four of Cups Tarot Card can reflect lost opportunities, guilt, or regret, in a general sense. It can also mean being self-absorbed because of depression, cynicism or apathy. The Four of Cups may mean you feel depressed or disillusioned with your life, and you may concentrate on the negative or feel like the grass on the other side is greener. You may feel like you've lost your love for life and motivation. When this Minor Arcana card appears in your Tarot spread, it comes with a warning that you should be aware of the possibilities or deals that are open to you. You may be inclined to dismiss them as trivial now, but you might later remember that they might have contributed to incredible stuff. The Four of Cups can also be a nostalgic, daydreaming, or fantasy look.

The Five of Cups

The Five of Cups shows a man in a long black cloak gazing down on three knocked-over cups- indicative of his deceptions and failures. Two cups standing behind him reflecting new possibilities and opportunity, but because he's so focused on his defeats (the spilled cups), he ignores the possibilities that he has to bring.

The Six of Cups

The Six Cups Tarot card is capable of reflecting love, childhood memories and past attention. If this card shows in a Tarot spread, you might be affected by past events. It may act as a symbol of the past or someone from your past. The Six of Cups is also the Minor Arcana card for babies, youth and youthfulness, and can signify having children or taking care of them or working with them. Simplicity, playfulness, kindness, goodwill and solidarity can be signified. It can represent defense, as well as family. When you've been through a hard time, the Six of Cups may be asking you to take the support from family and close friends. If the Six of Cups appears in a spread of Tarot, it can also mean that you are childish or immature. In certain cases, it may suggest childhood abuse when paired with other supporting cards. It can also mean homesickness for those who live outside the country.

The Seven of Cups

The Seven of Cups symbolizes creativity, desire, wishful thinking, fantasy and illusion. The card shows a person with his back turned to us, contemplating seven things creeping out of the cups, all of which float in the clouds. Clouds reflect visions, delusions, emotions, and fantasy. Several dreams are coming from the cups, which are symbolic of the many hallucinations you see while you sleep. The Seven of Cups might mean you've got several choices to make.

The Eight of Cups

We're faced with the transformation moment in the Eight of Cups. We see a cloaked man leaving behind eight golden cups to head off into a barren field. He's sick of all those cups that he's been collecting for so much time. He is now setting out to pursue a higher purpose. It can be the product of frustration or unhappiness that comes with knowing that something they've been striving for in life isn't as pleasurable or as rewarding as they once thought it would be.

The person who undertakes this journey may also be searching for excitement in the unknown. The desolate mountainous lands he sets off to can also be symbols of meeting new challenges. Their deep silence appears to mean that they are waiting for one to come to form it. The journey taken can be made in the form of trying out new ideas which have the potential to help one develop both mentally and spiritually. It also demonstrates the willingness to separate oneself from others so one can focus on self-improvement, self-understanding and development.

Nine of Cups

Often the Nine of this Suit is called Joy, but it is also known as Victory. The illustration on this card in many iterations also shows an innkeeper doing a good business and looking very pleased about it all. Nevertheless, the benefits of high achievement aren't just monetary. This joy also applies to the feelings of fulfilment that come from excellent service to the community and encouragement to one's family. It also shows as well as gratitude for all the blessings in one's life.

Ten of Cups

Traditionally, the Ten of this Suit represents family and community, sometimes displaying a celebratory scene involving several generations, topped with a rainbow signaling the end of hard times. See this dream compassion and support spreading in all directions for everybody, a massive emotional safety net.

The Page of Cups

The Page of Cups wears a blue robe with a floral pattern and a long, flowing scarf on his head with a beret. He stands on the beach, holding a cup in his right hand and the wavy sea behind him. Surprisingly, a fish pops out of the cup from its head and looks at the young man. Behind him, the fish and sea represent the dimension of Water and all things related to imagination, intuition, feelings and emotions. The fish's sudden presence means artistic inspiration always comes out of the blue, and only when you are open to it.

The Knight of Cups

The tarot card for the Knight of Cups represents something out of a storybook. A knight in armor is seated on a white horse with a golden cup in his hand. He's holding the cup out before him as if giving it to someone we can't see. This card's illustration reflects the traditional fairytale heroic knight riding in on a white steed to rescue the damsel in distress.

The Queen of Cups

The Queen of Cups rules over the world of feeling. She is the woman whose domain is right on the edge of the ocean, and water is usually a sign of the unconscious and the feeling. Her shore location means that she lies between land and sea, the place where there are feeling and thinking. She carries a cup which has an angel-shaped handle. This cup is closed, which is why the Queen of Cups symbolizes our unconscious mind. The Queen sits alone, allowing her to think. The quietness of the water and the sky symbolizes the Queen's serene mind.

Her feet do not touch the surface, which stands for her to look at her inner-thinking and feelings.

The King of Cups

The King of Cups is a tarot card which shows kindness, emotional balance and power. The card itself portrays a King sitting on a throne, with an amulet shaped like a shark. The fish in his necklace reflects his imagination and spirit, thriving on the calm waters around him. From the context, we can see that a constant balance occurs between the conscious and the unconscious. On the right side, a fish is jumping out of the ocean behind the King. There is a ship on the left side reflecting the emotional and material worlds, respectively. The King of Cups demonstrates you didn't curb your urges but learned to treat them in a controlled way.

Understanding the Suit of Pentacles

The Pentacle Suit represents the Earth dimension representing the physical objects such as money, company, properties, work, and creativity. The Suit of Pentacles in a reading represents the achievement of goals, the expression of success and prosperity.

Now we will look at the list of Minor Arcana cards from the Suit of Pentacles.

Ace of Pentacles

There is one single mystery hand coming out of the clouds in this card. In hand is what looks like a gold coin on its back, with a pentagram engraved. This pentacle is identified with the earth dimension. It is seen as a symbol of wealth and all material and worldly things. Below the hand is a lush garden with flowers and other kinds of plants-giving off the atmosphere of abundance, development and prosperity. The mountain represents the determination required for driving one's pentacle quest. The flowing creek seems to suggest that emotions flow toward that ambition.

Two of Pentacles

The Two of Pentacles card portrays a man dancing while holding two large coins. The pentacles are surrounded by the sign of infinity that signifies that the individual can handle all the issues that come his way and that he can gracefully manage his life. You'll note in the background that two ships are riding the giant waves, and they illustrate the juggling act the man has to face-he's in rough and choppy seas, but he manages to remain afloat. The Two of Pentacles is a representation of the regular ups and downs in one's life. For all the turmoil that surrounds him, as he dances, the man lives a very carefree life and manages with happiness all that comes to him.

Three of Pentacles

The Three of Pentacles depicts a young trainee working in a cathedral. There are two others in front of him, a priest and some nobleman, who keep cathedral plans on a piece of parchment. By the way, the apprentice lifted his head; we can tell that he is addressing his success in building the cathedral. The other two listen to him keenly to understand more clearly what is expected of them and how they can provide direction. Given the less experienced student, the other two listen to him as they know his ideas and his experience is essential for the successful completion of the entire house.

Therefore, the Three of Pentacles reflects the coming together of various kinds of experience to create something together.

Four of Pentacles

The Tarot Four Pentacles card can imply that you hang on to individuals, possessions, circumstances or past issues. It may be a sign that you need to process and let go of deeply rooted problems that concern you. This Minor Arcana card may mean that you may find it very difficult to stick to the people or things that offer you a sense of protection. You can hold on to stuff in such a way as to be unhealthy, possessive, controlling or harmful or someone can hold onto you. It may mean that you need to set limits or respect other people's boundaries. The Four of Pentacles may also suggest a lack of transparency, preventing or hindering development, keeping to yourself or isolating yourself. It can reflect money, greed, materialism and pinching of pennies.

The Five of Pentacles

As with the fives of the tarot's other sets, the Five of Pentacles symbolizes hardship. It shows two people walking out while snowing. They're not just cold; they're sick, weak, exhausted and hungry too. It seems like they lack the necessities of life. Many individuals can respond to the two in more ways than one. One of the card's individuals has crutches, and the other one has a shawl that covers her eyes. She runs in the snow, barefoot. In the background is a black wall with a stained glass window showing the five pentacles, which suggests some sort of church. The Five of Pentacles is more often than not an unfavorable omen. Do not fret, however, because it can change depending on where it is put in the reading.

Six of Pentacles

The Six of Pentacles is Pentacles' sixth card in their suit. A more positive card than the most recent Pentacles suit cards; things are beginning to look much more promising and are maturing now as well. It gives a message to try to see things as they are, to see how much of a positive difference you can make in the world.

Seven of Pentacles

A balanced card by definition the seven indicates you escape failure but in an attempt fall short of runaway success. Or, equally likely, you'll reach your goals, but not within the time frame you've expected. You'll face challenges, and you'll need to be vigilant to avoid being too reluctant or timid to succeed. Progress can be sluggish or hard, but it can be.

Eight of Pentacles

The Eight of Pentacles card depicts a young man etching into the eight golden coins a pentacle design. The card symbolizes someone completely concentrated and invested in what they do. The town far in the distance means he has effectively removed himself from the distractions so he can focus entirely on his mission. The Eight of Pentacles refers to those moments in your life when you're committed to completing some mission. You're fully engaged and dedicated to producing the best version of your work.

Nine of Pentacles

Nine of the tarot cards with Pentacles reflect luxury and financial stability. Often nine pentacles mean you're on a lavish holiday. It also means being surrounded by nature, like a flower, and living in an oasis of convenience. The energies of this tarot card are a comfortable home which soothes body, mind and soul. Nine of Pentacles often denotes someone who is a star instantly, at least on the surface, but there is still plenty of effort put into the subject that people don't see. If this card represents the Seeker, he/she will likely be self-sufficient and optimistic. If this card is in the role of advice, then take a break from work and enjoy beautiful scenery instead will offer you peace and harmony. Enjoy your life, and live your happy life. It gives you the energy you need to complete any unfinished tasks and jobs. Nine of Pentacles reminds us of maintaining grace and being tactful when dealing with others because this is the class and style card.

Ten of Pentacles

The Ten of Pentacles features an ancient, white-haired man wearing an ornamented robe, sitting at his feet with his two faithful white dogs. A younger couple with a small child stands nearby. The man is a prosperous father who has accomplished a great deal throughout his lifetime and is deeply gratified that he can now share with his loved ones his riches and abundance. His contributions and accomplishments now give his family financial stability and assurance. He can see the legacy which he has built already. The man and his family assemble at a large castle courtyard to display their wealth, comfort and financial stability. Family emblems and flags stand on the archway, a sign of their heritage and ancestors. Their wealth goes far beyond material comfort; they have a profoundly rooted link between the man and his family and their heritage, home and culture.

Page of Pentacles

The Page of Pentacles card shows a youth standing in a large field surrounded by flowers all by themselves. You'll also note some lush trees in the distance, and a furrowed plain. The young man appears to be strolling and is unaware of his surroundings, since his consciousness is entirely captured by the coin he carries, and all that it represents: ambition, stability, money, nature and sensuality. Pentacle Page symbolizes a rooted, faithful, and diligent human.

The Knight of Pentacles

The Pentacle Knight symbolizes the virtues of patience, honesty, and trustworthiness, and his appearance in your spread can also mean that you possess these traits. An alternate standard view is that he represents a young man, a trustworthy messenger of good news that will reach your life very soon.

The Queen of Pentacles

A woman sits on a stone seat in the Queen of Pentacles adorned with the carvings of fruit trees, goats, angels and other icons of material achievement and sensual pleasure. As if to cultivate this sign of riches and material prosperity, she cradles a gold coin with both hands and looks down upon it with loving care. It is surrounded by luscious plants and flowers, reflecting her relation to Mother Earth, nature and abundance. A tiny rabbit hops near where she sits, symbolizing vitality and indicating that her life is in harmony and flow.

The King of Pentacles

The King of Pentacles corresponds to a man of great ambition, materialistic contentment, and worldly achievement. The King of Pentacles sits on a throne decorated with vines and bull carvings, and many grapevine pictures embroider the robe he wears. He looks sophisticated and regal. He is also surrounded by various types of plants, vines, and flowers which depict the achievement of worldly success by this King. He is holding a scepter in his right hand, and a coin in his left hand with a pentacle graved on it. Behind him can be seen in the castle, which is a sign of his commitment and effort.

Understanding the Suit of Swords

The Suit of Swords portrays the element of air which represents the thoughts, beliefs and attitudes of a person. Within reading the signs of the Suit of Swords is always associated with determination, bravery, force, transition, strength and hardship.

Now we will look at the list of Minor Arcana from the Suit of Swords.

Ace of Swords

The Ace of Swords depicts a hand holding a double-edged sword rising from the clouds. This double-edged sword bears a golden crown and is surrounded by a wreath. The wreath has long been synonymous with prosperity, victory and great accomplishment. The crown is used as a sign of monarchy, and the ability to govern that comes with the monarchy. The sword is floating over a varied setting behind the foreground. It is carrying both mountains and sea, which are used as representations of the vast reach and distant lands that the swords will use to conquer, as well as determination.

Two of Swords

The Two of Swords symbolizes the uncertainty we face when we are forced to make hard choices. There is a seated woman in the Two of Swords game, who is blindfolded carrying a sword in her hands. In the context, there is a sea surrounded by rocks and crags that serve as barriers to boats and people, hampering development and practice. The blindfolded woman is a portrayal of a condition preventing her from seeing both the question and the solution.

Three of Swords

The tarot card Three of Swords reflects a time of emotional chaos. After drawing this card in a reading, you might know what it applies to. When you don't, this will act as a guide of what is yet to come. The reading foretells that life will throw your way through a curveball, and you'll be caught off guard, leading to heartbreak and hurt. This card also acts as a reminder to keep dear to your heart the things that you care about. Embrace those you love and share with them how you feel. Count your blessings, and know that a lovely rainbow falls at the end of every storm. You could get knocked down, but you're overcoming everything that comes along the way.

Four of Swords

The Four of Swords depicts a knight sitting horizontally on a grave. He remains in his full covering, and his hands are in the place of prayer as a sign of rest. One sword is lying under the knight, symbolizing a single focal point, and three swords are hanging over him, pointing downward to his head and chest. Over him, the stained-glass window depicts a woman and child together.

Five of Swords

The clouds which are irregularly shaped symbolize a time of strife. The two swords on the ground symbolize the two people are walking away from defeat. The two swords in the left hand of the man pointing up to express the competitive nature of the individual. The blade in his right-hand points downward and symbolizes the disparity that contributes to conflict—it deceits between the conscious and the subconscious.

Six of Swords

The Six of Swords depicts a woman and a small child being rowed across a body of water to the nearby countryside. Her head is veiled, indicating sorrow or disappointment in her life as she moves away from it. Her child is nestling near her body, finding protection and warmth as they begin this journey together. Six swords stand in the boat, indicating that the woman and child either hold memories or baggage from past to future. Although the water at the boat's right is rough, the sea ahead is calm. This picture suggests leaving a turbulent situation behind, heading for a more secure and welcoming climate.

Seven of Swords

The Seven of Swords depicts a man with five swords in his arms sneezing away from a military base. He looks at the two upright swords he has left behind, over his shoulder. The grin on his face shows he's proud of himself for slipping away without being heard.

Eight of Swords

The Eight of this suit, also called "The Test," usually portrays a fighter running the gauntlet, under intense examination, who finds out just how tough he or she is (or is not) in the process. Life gives us plenty of encounters that place us in scrutiny circumstances — whether it's an entrance test, a critical work interview or even the rough discussions that accompany a breach of confidence in a close relationship.

The Nine of Swords

The Nine of Swords is one from the cards of fear and anxiety in the Sword Suit. Like the other fear cards, this card is not an indicator of real adverse incidents, only that the level of fear and anxiety is so healthy that they make you believe things are worse than they are. In short, mountains can be built from molehills. It reflects tension, pressures, profound unhappiness and negative thought. You may feel exhausted and unable to deal with or face circumstances, challenges or even general life and may have hit your point of the break. It is a Minor Arcana card of agony, sorrow, shame, disappointment, joylessness and desperation and you may dream you could go back in time and rewrite the past as it happens. It can also mean feeling lonely and being the target of rumors and can reflect nightmares and sleeplessness.

Ten of Swords

Many of the most striking and threatening cards on the deck, the Ten of Swords shows a man lying flat on the ground facing the dirt. From the chest down to his knees, he is covered with a red fabric. Ten long swords are stabbed in his back; maybe he did not see the end coming. There's a horrible stillness in the air: the sky above him is black and gloomy, showing the death-related apprehension and negativity. The waters before him are still, without ripples-leading to this card's eerie quietness and finality. By looking through the horizon, the sun is rising in the east, and amid the darkness. The atmosphere seems very calm. The Ten of Swords appears to suggest this is the lowest point of one's life and things can't get worse than this. Even in this place, the sun rises, at least.

The Page of Swords

The Page of Swords card is symbolic of a person who shows an abundance of energy in one's life. A teenager stands confidently on a rugged precipice with wind-blown leaves, swirling clouds and their tossed heads. This enthusiastic young person has a sword in his hands. Her face is one of determination, and maybe a touch of defiance-she appears ready to pounce at the slightest sound.

The Knight of Swords

It is a change card, and it tells you there's a significant change coming, one you've been waiting for quite a while, and you'd better be able to roll with it when it does. It's time to spring in and enjoy the moment! It is a card of being assertive, straightforward, truthful, intelligent and humorous. It means being dashing, bold, adventurous, adventurous or rebellious. It also means being talkative, optimistic, forward-thinking, concentrated and one-minded as it appears in the spread of your Tarot. When this card comes in your Tarot reading, it can mean you are going against the flow, having great leadership qualities, and being a perfectionist and a risk-taker. The Knight of Swords is an adult (20-35 years old and typically male) with a strong personality who is quick-witted, a fast-talker, intelligent, daring and rebellious when representing a human. He may be an air symbol, like Aquarius, Gemini or Libra. The knight is reasonable and assertive but can be impatient and impulsive. He has a very blunt approach, and sometimes this may make him seem a little insensitive. He's fun and adventurous though, which draws people to him too. This card represents fighters, heroes and warriors heading into combat and as such, it may serve a soldier or anybody in the army.

The Queen of Swords

The Queen of Swords is sporting a stern look as she sits high on the throne-gazing into the distance. A queen of the air dimension depicted by the swords, her position in the clouds shows no-one can trick or confuse her. The sword she is carrying in her right hand is pointed toward the sky, while the left hand is held out like something is offered. In daily choices, the Queen of Swords gives us the gift of discretion and has the flexibility to take the experience from others.

The King of Swords

The tarot card of the King of Swords depicts a king seated on his throne while carrying a double-edged sword in his right hand pointing upwards. Intellectual strength, critical thought, honesty, and authority radiate from the King of Swords He knows that great responsibility lies with authority. The blue tunic the king wears is a symbol of his spiritual understanding. The butterflies at his throne's back suggest a change.

Understanding The Suit of Wands

The Suit of Wands represents the Fire dimension mirroring determination, spiritual inclination, power, behavior, creativity and power. The Suit of Wands represents the personality, passion and personal strength in a tarot card reading.

Now we will look at the list of Minor Arcana from the Suit of Wands.

Ace of Wands

Wands are synonymous with fire energy, and the Ace of Wands is the deck's intermediate representation of fire. The card depicts a hand which sticks out of a cloud while holding the wand. By looking at this card, we can see that the hand extends to give the wand, which is still that. Many of the wand leaves have sprouted which is supposed to signify spiritual and material equilibrium and development. In the distance is a castle which symbolizes future opportunities.

Two of Wands

The Two of Wands depicts a man carrying a small globe, dressed in a red robe and hat. If he can broaden his horizons accordingly, the universe is practically in his possession, marking the immense potential before him. He stands within the walls of his house, indicating that the man has not yet left his comfort zone to explore them while considering significant opportunities; he is still very much in the planning process. His hand rests on an upright wand, and a second wand is fixed to the wall of the castle, yet another indication that he is not ready to step out. The land is rich in the background but also rugged, promising to have a reasonable chance of success as long as it can resolve the obstacles that will arise.

Three of Wands

The Three of Wands shows a man standing on a cliff with his back turned, in red and green robes. Three wands stand firmly in the dirt, which reflects his devotion to his plans. He has left the castle's security in the Two of Wands and is now in a vast open space, gazing out to distant mountains over the sea. He sees three sailing ships passing by, symbolizing motion and development. He can see all that lies ahead from his elevated vantage point, including any obstacles and opportunities to come.

Four of Wands

Tarot's Four of Wands stands for joy, liberty and anticipation. It's all about growth and alliances, and it's about activities generating excitement. The excitement and the celebration could come as a surprise and be unexpected. Often the Four of Wands appearing in reading reflects a scheduled event, such as a wedding or anniversary. Those activities and festivities leave you with a feeling of joy. The enthusiasm is that of the little boy, still present in all adults, only waiting to get out. It is the children's joy when they see a birthday cake illuminated with candles; the kid waits for a turn on the roller coaster. The Four of Wands also stands for equality that can take several forms.

Five of Wands

The Five of this suit symbolizes the battle of aggressive maneuvering and competitive desire. It may be about someone moving forward his or her goals at the detriment of others.

Six of Wands

The Six of this suit points to your due respect and appreciation for your efforts to solve the community's problems. The picture is typical of a victory parade, having helped troops win a decisive battle after the revered chief.

Seven of Wands

The Seven of Wands shows a person who is almost always good at working his/her desire. It is a truly gifted guy, standing head and shoulders above the rest. This individual sets expectations and sets examples of what is possible that goes beyond previous conceptions.

Eight of Wands

The Eight of this suit shows a flight of spears or staffs moving in formation through the air. It shows as if a hidden party of archers had let them all move at once. It can apply to events quickly occurring, be it accidental or deliberate design. There is also a variety which emphasizes the agricultural cycle, parallel to the annual crop cycle with the rapid growth of children into adults with their own families.

Nine of Wands

Generally, the Nine of this suit shows a need for rest; some time off to mend wounds and savor the victory. Although it may be challenging to do, for now, this card will make you leave the field to fresher teammates. For now, release any commitment you might feel in a leadership position.

Ten of Wands

The Ten of this suit is an all-out effort, an obsessive dedication to a task which demands everything you have. The person seen in decks with pictures is in no position to rest until he makes it within the well-defended castle's rugged walls in the distance. Unless he fails, after dark he'll become prey to the highway robbers.

Page of Wands

This card is usually called The Page but appears as a Princess in some modern sets. This stereotype is the one of a particular person, a nonconformist, always something of a bohemian, by definition certainly autonomous. He or she needs no assertiveness or approval. Perhaps a mischief-maker, always an innovator or inventor, the energy that this card reflects can only serve others until he or she works out how to get others to help him/her.

Knight of Wands

This character is historically called the Knight but appears as the Prince in some modern decks. Traditionally, this card shows an instigator's strength, a fire-starter, a feisty and easily provoked character who is likely to strike and ask questions later initially. This energy is quick to get angry and loves a war — so much so that the thought of a peaceful solution can give rise to a hidden deception! Even, he sees himself as trying to improve,

Queen of Wands

Traditionally reflecting a Queen's strength, this woman represents the natural boss who has the gift of encouraging teamwork and divvying up tasks. She is the one who sees to ensure the smooth running of everything. She would sweat in the heat along with her family or friends, inspiring us with her infectious enthusiasm to keep up and boost morale.

King of Wands

This card is historically the strength of a powerful King and represents the classic conquering hero. He is a charismatic, enterprising and visionary leader often making new adventures. He does this because he does not like sitting at home or because he has to "run the shop" — he gets to feel frustrated and bored with the routine. He is your guy whether you need a crusader or someone to take on a significant challenge. He requires a big task and would prefer to lead rather than obey.

MINOR ARCANA

	WANDS	CUPS	SWORDS	PENTACLES
ACE	Creative Force Enthusiasm Confidence Courage	Emotional Force Intuition Intimacy Love	Mental Force Truth Justice Fortitude	Material Force Prosperity Practicality Trust
TWO	Personal Power Boldness Originality	Connection Truce Attraction	Blocked Emotions Avoidance Stalemate	Juggling Flexibility Fun
THREE	Exploration Foresight Leadership	Exuberance Friendship Community	Heartbreak Loneliness Betrayal	Teamwork Planning Competence
FOUR	Celebration Freedom Excitement	Self-Absorption Apathy Going Within	Rest Contemplation Quiet Preparation	Possessiveness Control Blocked Change
FIVE	Disagreement Competition Hassles	Loss Bereavement Regret	Self-Interest Discord Open Dishonor	Hard Times Ill Health Rejection
SIX	Triumph Acclaim Pride	Good Will Innocence Childhood	The Blues Recovery Travel	Having/Not Having: Resources Knowledge Power
SEVEN	Aggression Defiance Conviction	Wishful Thinking Options Dissipation	Running Away Lone-Wolf Style Hidden Dishonor	Assessment Reward Direction Change
EIGHT	Quick Action Conclusion News	Deeper Meaning Moving On Weariness	Restriction Confusion Powerlessness	Diligence Knowledge Detail
NINE	Defensiveness Perseverance Stamina	Wish Fulfillment Satisfaction Sensual Pleasure	Worry Guilt Anguish	Discipline Self-Reliance Refinement
TEN	Overextending Burdens Struggle	Joy Peace Family	Bottoming Out Victim Mentality Martyrdom	Affluence Permanence Convention

3.3 Trusting Your Intuition

Have you found that bookstores are full of self-help books, but there aren't too many to illustrate how your intuition can be extended? It is because there is no reliable measure of skill or development, but mainly because practice is the only way to learn.

That wouldn't make the book very exciting (or long)! You've heard the saying, "Trust your gut." It is truly the only way your intuition will develop. Trust that. The single real measuring stick of intelligence is your self-trust and self-esteem. Only trust your instincts. What most of you might have encountered is a perfect example of intuition. A mother with no rational thinking realizes that her missing child is on her way home, or worse, injured. Have you ever met a mom doubting her knowledge? No, they recognize that and they act on it. It is often used as an example, simply because this scenario is the most popular. Parents are profoundly attuned to their children and are so deeply involved in their daily lives that the intuitive (psychic) connection is profound. Through nature itself, a mother is compelled to trust the emotion, to ensure humanity survives. Even then, they'll probably always tell you they're not intuitive or psychic. The reality is we are all, but some are more developing, trusting, and exercising their instincts. Your intuition is recognizing that your best friend is calling to ask a stranger in line at the grocery store until the phone rings and extending your intuition is taking the knowledge a few steps further. Always be respectful by not prying into the lives of others who don't agree to you. I think reading the Tarot is a perfect resource for learning how to trust, practice and calculate your abilities. We are just two cards into the deck when we are told by the High Priestess to be calm, quiet and to look inside. The High Priestess demands you have faith and belief in what you know. Trust your instincts, trust your heart and gain information. Don't consider yourself second. You must believe in intangible things, and be able to admit that you know what you have not experienced, but understand. Don't be confined to logic and reason, or rational thought.

Yes, Tarot cards have traditional significances, and learning them is necessary. There are 78 cards, all with meaning to know, but, depending on several factors, the meanings shift, somewhat. It's a difficult job to learn these. Practice and trust your intuition are the keys to reading The Tarot. The Tarot is a perfect way to expand your insight into certain aspects of your life. The Tarot asks you to search in their photos for a story. It is a story that relates to the life of the questioner. Getting faith in the story requires courage then. One preparation in the morning involves drawing a single card. For this exercise, it's not necessary to know its conventional meaning; in fact, it is best to help your intuition develop if you do not know the meaning or can put the meaning aside. It is the trust that is what you need. What does the card say you? What is it that tells you about your day? Is it an entity, and do you know them? Would you want to try them out, or stop them? Will they demand your attention, or are they busy in their world? Would you have to mimic their behavior, or be careful of those who do so? Maybe the picture represents good things in your day or warns of a problem that needs to be resolved or avoided. Write down this and put it out of your mind, and put away the card and paper. It can be challenging to do, but try. By the end of the day, revisit your card and your writing. Compare the observations with the day. Is your impression right about its message? I trust it does.

I think the best readings are those where people allow their psychic intuition to light Tarot cards up.

Enlist a few volunteers and give free Tarot readings for them. Typically, if you charge, giving free readings will take off the pressure to perform and encourage you to try a new approach.

Until you read the Tarot, set your mind to activate your intuition by everything you do - to shuffle, to cut, or spread out the cards.

With your psychic intuition, you can filter what the cards mean. Use it to say the difference between a generalization of something that might happen to anyone, something that is not important and something that you know is a success.

Then, begin to talk. At first, you could wobble, like Dumbo stuttering in the air as he lost his magic feather. But as soon as he realized he didn't need it, he soared, and as you learn to trust your psychic instincts, that's what you will do too.

3.4 Combination of Cards

As you begin reading tarot for the first time, your main emphasis is on discovering the meanings of the individual card and spreading the positions. But even though you start to feel confident with the fundamentals, you'll still get stuck on one thing: how to grasp variations of tarot cards. It is a topic that I have seen pop-up in various tarot groups and forums several times. You certainly aren't the only one to ask the question: "How do I view combinations of tarot cards? I may grasp them separately, but I'm stumped when it comes to bringing them together in a read! "You may be so used to reading cards individually when you go through a set, that it may seem quite confusing and difficult to understand when it comes to understanding pairings of two or more cards in combination. I'm here to tell you this isn't as hard as you might imagine!

It gets much easier to understand until you learn the right tips and tricks. I'll share some of my latest advice on knowing tarot card combinations with you here.

Is Tarot Combination Helpful for You?

I know you're probably searching for a list of tarot combinations, or some service you can link to. Yet, it would be such a waste of your energy. Why? For what? Ok, consider this: A deck includes 78 cards, right? Which means which each card contains 77 potential pairings. That's more than 3000 potential mergers! You tell me now, how do you remember all of that? Not to mention the fact that you might not even apply the combined sense you read in the book or app to your case! The meanings of the card change, depending on the querent's question and circumstance. Knowing how to mix each card pairing is much more useful than attempting to memorize all the combinations! When you want to take the readings beyond the meanings of a single card, I find that an invaluable ability.

Synergy is the Key

The first advice I would like to give you about how to interpret card combinations is the synergy theory. Synergy is the concept that the unbroken is better than the sum of its parts. Therefore, one plus one is equivalent to three instead of two as the end product is something unique and different from its pieces. When it comes to combinations of tarot cards, synergy is when the interpretation of two or more cards creates a cumulative meaning more significant than the total of the meanings of the individual cards. You want to strive for that when reading combinations of cards. To further highlight this point, let's presume you have a two-card pairing. When you perceive their definitions independently from each other, absolutely it doesn't count as synergy.

When you seek to understand pairings of two or more cards, there is a danger that you may slip into the trap of this old practice of first interpreting one's card, and then card the trap of two. Second, and then, this set of keywords. That's not what you want this place to go for. You want to consider the difference between the first card's definitions and the second card's. It is about teamwork! Instead of looking at the two cards separately, ask yourself what special significance do those cards have in common? When you combine the keywords for card one with those of card two, what is the meaning that you can't come up with when you look at them individually? It could be hard to do at first. My tarot tutor used to quiz me on these card combinations, years ago. She would pose two-card combinations and then ask me to think of a definition in combination. If she thought the sense I provided was not very special, she would ask me to do the exercise again! It took me some time to learn this so what I encourage you to do is practice reading card combinations just as I did and don't panic if at first, you find it challenging to think of a combined sense. If you get the hang of it, it will get easier!

Look at the Dynamics between the Cards

The second suggestion I have for you is thinking about the dynamics between the cards that you have drawn. Tarot cards are not required to be read in standalone form. They do not live in a vacuum!

Tarot meanings influence each other and how they communicate with each other depends on your understanding of any given card or group of cards.

Ask yourself this while you're contemplating card combinations:

- Do the cards reinforce each other?
- Do they feed on one another?
- Are they trying to have a similar meaning?
- Should they stand in opposition to each other?
- Are they meetings opposite to the tarot card?
- Are they merely dichotomous?
- Are card significances equivalent to one another?

Your answer to these questions determines how you view the cards and what inference you draw from the reading.

You put greater emphasis on the combined context if they complement one another.

If they contradict each other, you'll put more emphasis on the card indicating differences.

If they're neutral, you can read them as a standard combination of cards without any specific emphasis.

Examples of Tarot Card Combinations

I know all of this may still sound a little vague to you, so that's why I've prepared a couple of examples to highlight the points I've described.

After all, Examples are the best way to know!

The Sun and the Magician

It is a mix of cards, in which I believe the meanings of the card certainly go together and feed one another.

You've got The Sun which is a card about happiness, victory, achievement, and light. And then you have The Magician, a card which is all about determination, motivation, transformation, and making things happen. By putting it together, my understanding is that it alludes to the Law of Attraction together. It is universal energy in practice, especially considering the sign of infinity on The Magician and the energy of light in The Sun. I should make sure that I stress the Law of Attraction in a reading.

The Sun and the Four Swords

I believe this combination of cards is a little neutral to one another. They are not especially supporting or challenging one another. So, you depend on synergy alone in this case and do not need to stress its meaning more than other parts of your reading. The Sun is a very luminous card. It is packed with light, and it is taken by many people to mean spreading the light around the world. It has very masculine, critical, projective energy too. Four of Swords generally means rest and recuperation. Some wanted a lot of downtimes. My personal view is that it points to a potential burnout connected to stress together. It is someone who has given the world so much of himself and who just needs to take some time off to regain the precious strength.

The Sun and the Moon

The Sun and the Moon are classic opposites, and as such, you should put greater focus on their differences when reading them together. The Sun, as I said, is the projective energy, strength, beauty, happiness, and prosperity. By contract, the Moon has very receptive energy, and it reminds of the night's stillness. Reflection, visions, psychic powers, sleep, dreams, and intuition are all about. When you bring together these two words, note they are opposing each other! What I see in this combination of cards is an emotional difference between a yin and yang force. I see the need to realign one's resources, and where the disparity depends on which card the eye is first drawn to. So, first assuming my eye is attracted to The Light, then I'd think the imbalance is in favor of Yang energy. There is much male energy and needs to be balanced by the querier with the correct time for reflection.

If, on the other hand, I'm more attracted to The Sun, I'd say the imbalance is in favor of Yin power. There is so much reflective, feminine, emotion, and the questioner needs to get a bit out of his mind. Excessive Yin can hinder them from acting to spread their light or prevent them from experiencing happiness. Remember, there is no wrong answer here. When reading those cards, people will have a different idea. How do you think of these combinations of three cards and maybe your definition is different from mine? If so, then I want to know what you think!

You can Practice Card Combination at Home

Drawing two cards and talking about the combined sense is something you can do at home with ease! Only shuffle your deck, pick up a pair of cards and then ask yourself: what do these two cards mean? If you have difficulty finding the particular synergistic sense, then I suggest you make a list of the first card keywords, a list of the second card keywords. Choose two main terms, one for each card, and draw a line in between. Then ask yourself: if I mix this keyword with this keyword. What is the third keyword I'm able to come up with is a particular consequence of the two others? It is a straightforward exercise that you can do every day if you so choose and be confident you won't run out of combinations! After all, there are over 3000 of those! And it would take you like eight years before you run out of card combinations, even though you do this exercise every day. You will keep yourself practically amused for such a long time! I hope these two easy tips and tricks that I gave you have helped to shed light on the subject of card combinations. Try the exercise that I suggested and share how it works with me!

3.5 The Meaning of Numbers and Colors in Tarot World

Occasionally it is easy to overlook the numerical value of tarot cards in readings or general contemplation. The Tarot is filled with meaning, and its numbers are often taken for granted as an essential cataloguing tool until a whole new world of mysticism and technique is finally opened up. To grasp the Tarot's energy better, we must consider all its facets, including its numerological perspectives. Numbers exude vibrations resonating with all the force and strike individual chords on the Universe's harp strings. By observing the numbers falling in a spread of the Tarot, we can pluck those vibrational strings and ring out from a reading further truth. The number value of Tarot cards at its purest will provide extra light for a tricky array. Such numerical definitions can also offer a different perspective when looking for solutions with the cards.

Number sense of Tarot cards at its most complex can blossom into incredible oracles of symmetry, geometry, and startling congruence that give us a fascinating accuracy in our readings. When you deal with the Tarot, begin to hone in on the numbers drawn to you. By using the reference number definition below to help you draw deeper meanings of your Tarot readings. Remember that the Tarot numerology method (or any numerology in that respect) reduces numbers. When you have drawn the Temperance card (14 of the major arcana) to demonstrate, you must the number to 5 because one plus four are equal to five.

Several Tarot numerology practitioners have chosen not to decrease the numbers at all. They are using the second digit as the numerical meaner, instead. For example, the Temperance card (14) is defined numerically by number 4. If you want to double the digits or pick the second digit as the numerical meaner, the readings will see impressive discoveries and increases. You can find that numbers are a puzzle with your knowledge of numerical meanings, as you can see that they allow for elasticity in your readings while simultaneously providing a grounding effect.

Have fun using this additional dimension of Tarot awareness, and enjoy the sources below for number sense.

Zero: Start and Ending, Alpha and Omega, Limitless, Infinite, Simple Will, Unity.

One: Freedom, Practice, Inspiration, Objective Individuality, Motivated, Positivity, Will.

Two: equilibrium, comparison, relationship, contact, negotiation, choice.

Three: Time, imagination, mobility, mystery, insight, fruitfulness and development

Four: Flexibility, strength, practicality, physicality, success, modesty, simplicity

Five: Movement, Erratic, Love, Adventure, Growth, Travel, Unpredictability

Six: Creation, Sincerity, Security, Sensitivity, Dependability, Growth, Nurturing.

Seven: Beauty, Creativity, Consciousness, Mysticism, Understanding, Healing.

Eight: Opportunity, Observation, Intention, Abundance, Repeat, Infinity.

Nine: Dream, Creativity, Control, Force of Intelligence, Achievement, Anticipation.

Color of Tarot Cards

In our Tarot interpretations, the meanings of colors in Tarot cards serve as the rubies, emeralds, and sapphires that glisten with clarity. To our intuition, each Tarot card is a treasure chest. Much like the Tarot's number meanings, the meanings of the colors in the cards bring our spreads a fresh new perspective. Even the earliest Tarot decks were very brightly colored, such as the Marseilles

Tarot. It's no mistake. It is understood that bright colors stimulate our subconscious and activate our intuitive minds.

It is brilliant to use colors in Tarot decks-it, stimulates our imagination and encourages our spirits to interact with the energies surrounding our readings. Understanding the meanings of colors will allow you to dive deeper into the information held by the Tarot. It will also enrich your interpretation of the Tarot and your appreciation for the interpretive arts.

When you experiment with the meanings of colors in the Tarot, do not hesitate to consult the following color importance map as a loose guide.

Red: Think of fire and blood- Red runs to us with passion signals, primitive desires, movement, joy, vibration, radiance, and love.

Orange: An excellent relaxed mix of violent red and yellow high-pitch. Orange is about unity, hope, sociability, contentment and intelligence.

Yellow: Worshipped in the shape of the Sun-Yellow is about oozing imagination, security, intelligence, positivity and clarity.

Green: Spring's fresh start brings Green oceans and with it comes youth qualities, sentimentality, nature, adventure, development and health.

Blue: Look to heaven for Blue's meanings-open spaces, independence, creativity, growth, motivation, and responsiveness.

Indigo: It has qualities similar to the of blue, but the energy of Indigo runs very deep. You can consider the unknown depths of the sea together with passion, power, fluidity, persuasiveness, expressiveness and omnipresence.

Violet: Violet, the color of delicate flowers and peaceful sunsets, reminds us of faith, communion, grandeur, values, commitment and harmony.

Brown: Anyone who has squashed their toes through the rich, moist earth has brown down-groundedness, earthiness, concrete, realistic, energetic, caring, and solidity, excellence, high ideals, devotion, and peace.

Gray: As fog rolls in and we're surrounded by Gray's haze, we understand his message- ambiguity, neutrality, confusion, strength, and austerity.

Black: Black is needed to have depth and variance of hue in all other colors. It is a powerful feature and reflects formality, modesty, intensity, convention, stability, and zero tolerance.

White: Contemplate the beauty of fresh white snow and how it throws a blanket of harmony over everything it touches. White stands for love, purification, salvation, integrity, innocence and the highest kind of understanding.

3.6 Which Tarot Cards Are Considered Good?

As far as the luckiest Tarot cards are concerned, every decent fortune teller can clarify that no card is automatically good or evil, depending on how closely you want to listen to their lessons. That said, in almost every reading, there are a few Tarot cards which indeed appear to be a welcome sight. Some of these cards carry fortune-coming news while others claim you're on the right track when it comes to love or money. Some readers bring some Tarot cards for good luck if there is anything that they're seeking to manifest in their lives in particular.

Now we'll look at a couple of these lucky tarot cards and what messages they may try to tell you when they appear in reading in different positions. Keep in mind that while the tarot may be an excellent indication of what will happen if you continue on a particular road, there is nothing like a future written in stone. Although a card will remind you that you are on the right track toward your goals, it is up to you to remain on that track before your dreams become a reality.

Though we have discussed all the cards earlier for elaborating the point to you, we will describe these.

Ace of Pentacles

The Ace of Pentacles features a large hand that stretches out from the clouds and over a lush, bountiful garden, giving the seeker a pentacle. A path is provided through the garden, which leads to higher ground. As a rule, Pentacles' suit stands for material abundance, prosperity, energy, and chance.

Ace of Cups

The Ace of Cups features a hand that carries a big, overflowing cup from the clouds. As the cup overflows into a large pool, a dove descends to it, taking Divine blessings with it.

Three of Cups

A fun little card shows three ladies as they dance in the middle of a bountiful field, with their cups held high. Bliss flows through the heart of the scene as they enjoy some champagne, each other's company and the food in hands.

The Sun

This card is filled with Color, Innocence and Honesty metaphors. The unclothed child symbolizes childhood happiness, innocence and independence while the horse stands for pureness and power.

The Lovers

Happiness is in the air when you see the card appearing in a reading. And not only a solely sensual relationship, but one in which you have found a real bond with another person giving both physical and emotional fulfilment.

The Star

If you have been through a rough time, then The Star's presence in reading is proof that time of renewed hope and intent is about to come.

Six of Wands

This card offers the promise of success and progress, while at the same time encouraging you to trust in your faith.

Ten of Cups

If you have always dreamed of a happier life at home, then the chances are high that when this card comes in your reading, it's coming your way.

The World

It's always a sign of progress, harmony, and fulfilment when this card comes in.

Nine of Pentacles

If you are a woman, if you pursue your dreams, this card might represent what you're supposed to become.

King of Pentacles

It shows that success is not far behind.

Empress

This card shows, it presents abundance in your life.

Which Cards Aare Considered Bad Cards?

Tarot readers suggest we're picking the cards we want to see. That's all well when they're optimistic cards, but what a lot of readers don't say is questions, but there are certain cards you never want to see in a tarot reading. These dark tarot cards show us something that we might already know is inside of us, whether it's an unhealthy attachment, deception, or inability to face a situation's true. Although seeing these cards that help us confront those facets of our lives that we have been avoiding for a long time, it does not make it any less disturbing to see them in a set.

Occult readers are quick to point out that the names of these cards don't automatically indicate the fate of a querent. Pulling the Devil card, for example, doesn't mean a supernatural entity can wreak havoc in your life, and the Death card doesn't mean you're going to wreck drastically in the next 24 hours! The most frightening cards to see in a tarot spread are figurative and keep our inner demons in a mirror, training us to make significant changes in our lives.

The Ten of Swords

This dreary small number shows a man facing down with ten swords plunging in his back. He has pulled back a red cloak, and heavens above him are always dark and foreboding. The 10 of Swords certainly isn't a positive one to turn over. The card can historically be viewed in a few ways, generally ranging somewhere between reaching the rock bottom, feeling helpless or humiliated, or somehow being deceived. To this trend of "bottoming out" there is a silver lining, or at least that is how some seers believe. Nothing to go but up from whatever condition the card applies to, whether it's a sudden loss, natural disaster, financial woes or illness. Yet this card's place in your spread changes its meaning. If the 10 of Swords land in your spread's "future" role, it means that you still have to hit the worst of something, and you should prepare for possible disruption or catastrophe.

The Tower

Although the name seems relatively innocuous, the Tower is pretty foreboding. The card shows a gloomy, stormy sky as a backdrop and in the foreground is a fiery, lightning-struck tower. Two men fell from the roof. The card displays a sudden shift or release which might have left you blindsided. The release can be anything from uncovering a secret truth to getting a revelation which changes life. The Tower Card is unusual in that its strength resides in the present; the place it falls in refers to where the shift lightning bolt comes from to shake you up. For instance, if it lands in the past place, it means the origins of the upheaval have already happened, and only now are the consequences of your life taking hold.

Three of Swords

This card shows Three of swords, in a red heart. As soon as you turn it over, this card looks like trouble. If you pull the 3 of Swords, it might mean you've endured some heartbreak or pain recently (or are in for it). If you're walking in with someone else on your lover or finding out a good friend has betrayed you, the Swords 3 reflects heartbreak, isolation and deceit. When drawn in the future location, it can be a valuable warning. Don't forget this card, though, might also mean you've caused such pain to someone else. Beware that you are pulling this wallet, and think long and hard about the business you are holding.

Nine of Swords

There are less more daunting pains to face than those we make for ourselves. Swords 9 reflects these kinds of pressures that we're bringing with us. During the night, the figure on the card is seen hunched over, as if worried, symbolic of the standard time these thoughts torment us and keep us awake. Yes, the Swords 9 is a card of misery, fear, anxiety and remorse. When you pull this card, it can mean that you've done something wrong and you're well aware of that. It is a card which means it's time for some introspection and discussing aspects of your life where you could change your behavior. You may have had an affair, cheated at test, or lied about something important. The nine of Swords reveals shame weighs heavily on you, and its time to make good your mistakes.

Death

This card depicts a skeleton knight bearing a black flag on a white horse as the character rides through a wasteland. It is an unsettling card to pull, even for readers with the most experience. Tarot readers are swift to remind the poor souls who pull this card that they will not be struck down by lightning the second they step out of the door; instead, the card is also associated with a life-altering or wrenching transition. The end of a friendship, a significant loss, getting fired from your job-all of these are possibilities, mainly if the card is in the place to come. One thing stressed about this game, though, is that it's impossible to fight. Readers say the imminent break or failure of your life is likely to happen after this card is pulled, so it's best to brace yourself for getting through it.

The Devil

The Devil's symbol is commonly associated by most of the world as something inherently evil, and those new to tarot can panic in the sight of this demonic beast. Although this card doesn't precisely mean something diabolical, the fact that this is not a card you want to see in your spread isn't getting around. The Devil means some destructive relationship in your life, whether it is with another person or with a drug. Under the beast, the man and woman chained together represent lust and shamelessness, referring to the recklessness with which you follow other relationships in your life.

Ten of Wands

It is a fighting card; a hint that you are in over your head. Whether in your profession or a personal relationship, this card means that you can have more off than you can chew. It means that you are in for a difficult period and that every day will be a little tougher than usual.

The Moon

The Moon Card, master of moods and tides, probably contains two meanings. It can reflect knowledge and enlightenment, or it can point to misunderstanding and strife. The Moon points to transition, emotional instability and confusion. When you pull this card, your worries or areas of your life in which you lack clarification that needs to be evaluated and dealt with.

The Hanged Man

With this card, one thing is obvious: It's about putting yourself in an awkward place where fighting won't help you. Instead, you have to let go, knowing that you cannot fight.

The Fool

The Fool is simply a footless and fancy-free attitude; you don't know what others think of you anymore, and you're going to do what makes you feel beautiful, whatever the possible consequences.

The Hermit

The Hermit card portrays an old hooded man carrying a lighted lantern, gazing into the distance. It's a very enigmatic deck card, which can carry various meanings. Throughout traditional lore, a hermit is someone who has turned away from the world voluntarily throughout search of answers and warmth inside their isolation.

A reversed card brings something of a surprise to the reading. It'll pull you up momentarily and make you pay attention. It will add extra complexity to the reading and maybe help you find a more precise explanation than it would have been if it were right. The more negative connotations of a card are easy to ignore if you see the good ones.

3.7 Reading of Reversed Tarot Cards and Their Meanings

Do you have any grasp of the Tarot card's fundamentals? All right, then you're set for reversals! Many experienced Tarot readers often shuffle their decks to include reversed Tarot cards, as they can provide another layer of insight. Turned upside down, the Tarot cards may have a purpose entirely different from their upright representations. Some people think a Tarot card that is reversed guarantees lousy news, but that is not the case at all. Reversed Tarot cards often bring good news, or strengthen, weaken, or redirect the upright card's original message. You must listen to your gut when reversed cards appear in your Tarot reading and look at the accompanying cards to get what the reversed Tarot card is trying to explore you. It can be positive, negative, or neither, it may merely convey a lesson that you need to learn. A reversed card brings something of a surprise to the reading. It'll pull you up momentarily and make you pay attention. It will add extra complexity to the reading and maybe help you find a more precise explanation than it would have been if it were right. The more negative connotations of a card are easy to ignore if you see the good ones.

Major Arcana Reversed Cards Meaning

- **Fool:** Make stupid decisions. Take positive advice aside. Got together with the wrong crowd.

- Magician: Trickery, deceit, evil. Scammer, scammer. Disorders of personality, for example narcissism. Lacking empathy.

- **High Priestess:** Originating from depression. Extreme shyness or over-confidence, denying instincts, sexual predatory behavior, superficiality, exposing of secrets.

- **Empress:** Hunger, and drought. Denied ground. Long live through your babies, smother-love. Vanity, empty nest syndrome, sense of uselessness, infidelity, hate, unsupportive. Questions concerning fertility. Company fails. Adoption problems or step-parenting issues.

- **Emperor:** Regulated Design. Urban sprawl and worsening. Authoritarian, ruler, dictator, tyranny, rigid, unyielding, issues with fatherhood, lack of authority, obstruction, abuse of power.

- **Hierophant:** Establishment rebuttal. A trainer with reasons beyond. Expulsion, being excommunicated. Sexual harassment. Inappropriate behavior. Rejecting one's convictions.

- **Lovers:** Inappropriate contact. Immaturity, loss of affection, possessiveness, stalking/infatuation, lust and not passion. Bad choice, indecision, temptation, vulnerability, loss of faith, detachment. Endless obsessive pursuit of non-existent soul-mate.

- **Chariot**: Ambition but at an expense. Real life has been disrupted. Problems with flying. Heat, quarrels, delays, injuries. Negotiations failed.

- **Strength:** Mental trouble. Too poor or overbearing. Not understanding when it is time to quit. Administration vs residents. Cruel. Disregard for other people's well-being to fulfill your wish.

- **Wheel of Fortune**: Better luck and bad. Fate, confusion and uncertainty.

- **Justice:** Upset about being lonely. Social isolation, anxiety, anguished identity crisis. Are concerned about aging. Fear of being dependent on others

- **Hanged Man:** Getting ready to go but holding off. Hidden goals or motivations. Job or tasks left unfinished. About moving on from a relationship or a friendship.

- **Death:** Tentative of preventing an imminent end. Chronic disease. Extreme pessimism or depression. Return from the

Dead. Death-obsession. Accident (with death barely escaping).

- **Temperance:** Non-cooperation, opposing ideas / views, out of alignment. Extreme feelings. Dysfunction. Problems of digestion. Healthy mind / body out of whack.

- **Devil:** Extremes of the upright meaning: psychopathic personality disorder, life-threatening addiction. Abuse (physical and mental); Escape, free, move on, take control of your problems and your future.

- **Tower:** Extremes of the upright meaning: psychopathic personality disorder, life-threatening addiction. Abuse (physical and mental); Escape, free, move on, take control of your problems and your future.

- **Star:** Self-esteem is low. Lack of accountability. Futile. Not feeling the love that is around you. Deep frustration.

- **Moon:** Resistance to spiritual stuff. Its self-deception. Locked attitude. Problems in mental health, and issues like problems with fibromyalgia and urinary tract.

- **Sun:** Weakened Upright Card capacity. Nevertheless, constructive but less so. Performance is very average. At a smaller scale, joy.

- **Judgment:** Transitions which are troublesome. Resistance, rejection, isolation. Critical and judgmental over.

- **World:** Upright card energy slightly decreased, but mostly positive. Completing unfinished programs. Wanting to move on but holding off. Overdue childbirth. Issues around weight loss. Waiting for test results.

Minor Arcana

- **Ace of Wands:** Depleted, straight-forward capacity. Inappropriate allure / affair. Lack of growth and spread.

- **Two of Wands:** Unanticipated turn of events. A new way of looking at an old issue. Reluctance, constraint placed on itself.

- **Three of Wands:** Feeling trapped. Unable to get underway or finished programs. Performance lagged behind. Anxiety over savings.

- **Four of Wands:** — Not much the reverse of upright. Celebration, parties, a break from hard work. Creating pillars, cementing partnerships. Land selling

- **Five of Wands: They are** refusing to commit to hostilities or conflict. They have difficulty to settle disputes—conflicts inside, beset by inner demons.

- **Six of Wands:** Crime, treason. The short-lived victory. Pride ahead of drops. Humiliating. Humiliation in general.

- **Seven of Wands:** Throwing down walls, refusing to compromise. Stubborn. Set.

- **Eight of Wands:** Unpredictable, challenging case. Terror. Terror. Problems with the family or company. Speak of the reversal as a baby brother of the Tower.

- **Nine of Wands:** Overcrowded. Ready to leave. Nagging pain, sickness. Unable to see the trees go.

- **Ten of Wands** -Hard labor: few results. Giving up a target or a dream. Facing a hard reality.

- **Page of Wands:** Childishness, tannery. Concentration and dedication are missing. Unfortunate news in the form of a letter or a reprimand.

- **Knight of Wands:** A thief, a consumer, a philanderer. A scoundrel. A cheater. A cheater. Over-enthusiasm, fearlessness, bad temper. Sensitive to attack.

- **Queen of Wands:** Another friend. A temperamental, jealous mistress. A love rival, or job competitor. Extravagance, promiscuity. Fever, with infections.

- **King of the Wands:** Greedy manager or dictator. Illuminated ego. Misuse of may. All-Powerful shows of rage. Heart attacks or subsequent stroke

The Suit of Cups

- **Ace of Cup:** Like to seep free. Setting limits on emotion. Forgotten or unrequited passion. Change in a Romantic to Routine relationship. Possible difficulty in drinking.

- **Two of the Cups:** Trouble communicating romantically. Using Obstacles. In the friend-zone, find yourself. Touch perishing. Separation.

- **Three of Cup**: Over-indulgence. Bored with drinking. They are Tucked away with close friends. Lack of support or cooperation.

- **Four of Cup**: Ready to surmount depression. Looking for answers. Getting ready for the transition. Intolerance. Slight insomnia. Fatigue, apathy. Psychic experiences.

- **Five of Cups**: Rifts to heal. Lessing the sadness. Aid from loved ones and friends. Acknowledgement.

- **Six of Cups**: Concern for the past or the future; They inability to live in the moment. Problems with a young person or a pet.

- **Seven of Cups**: Resolving sensations of doubt and uncertainty. Taking a proactive decision. Trust your sentiments.

- **Eight of Cups**: Home Going. The return of the Prodigal. Ave family acknowledged and welcomed. Met with a moral dilemma.

- **Nine of Cups**: Upright Card capacity diminished. It can reduce content or transient satisfaction. Letting go of concrete questions. Overcoming Errors. Food and Alcohol overindulgence.

- **Ten of Cups:** Difficulties in relation or relatives. Completion, which is challenging to reach. Break up or breakdown of a once happy house.

- **Page of Cup:** Teens suffering emotional distress. A possible misunderstanding over gender. Someone who fears love or emotional engagement. The young adult who doesn't fit in with family. An emotional message, and probably upsetting.

- **Knight of Cup:** Deceitful in love. Infidelity. Obsession with another guy. Problems of the LGBT or celebrations. Out coming.

- **Queen of Cups:** A very responsive lady. Maybe with health conditions and emotional issues. One who wants support both physically and emotionally. Withdrawal of a partner's love.

- **King of Cups:** A guy emotionally alone. Possible drug addict, or alcoholic. Depression and self-doubt cause problems in the relationship. Incapable of voicing personal feelings.

The Suit of Swords

- **Ace of Swords**: Patience, discipline. The block of the writer. Conceiving. Infringement. Work.

- **Two of Swords:** Ripped in two directions. Victim of deception, fraud, duplicity. Pared to make a call.

- **Three of Swords:** Quick recovery until the suffering breaks up or masks the actual severity of it.

- **Four of Swords:** Unintended isolation. Insomnia: Insomnia. Lack of self-restraint. They have strange dreams; felt out of shape.

- **Five Swords:** Upright card Weakened or magnified strength. Funeral: Funeral. Dying for conditions or men.

- **Six of Swords:** Wanting to escape but not being able to. Delays in travel, or cancellations. Floods, floods, power outages.

- **Seven of the Swords:** Shame on cheating or deceiving Giving back that which is not yours. Support to the Society. Giving in or paying in.

- **Eight of the Swords:** A common future dream. Capable of looking ahead. Hard job but satisfying.

- **Nine of Swords:** Depression-recovery. Opened up for new ideas. Ready to discuss options.

- **Ten of Swords:** Restoration, Recovery, Easement. The ending was not as bad as it seemed. Nouveau horizon.

- **Page of Swords:** Slanderous, bitter gossip. Childhood rough. Disorders of personality.

- **Knight of Sword:** fanatic. Fundamental. Cruel. Bad news arrives by email or by phone.

- **Queen of Swords:** Self-centered, deceptive woman. Narrow-mindedness, intolerance, bigotry
- **King of Swords:** Dangerous, naughty man. Command and exploitation. Cruel, inhumane and evil.

The Suit of Pentacles

- **Ace of Pentacles:** Excessive Upright Card capacity. Treasure, wealth and prosperity. Bliss less wealth. Obsessed about money-making. Fraud: Fraud. Come fast, go fast.
- **Two of the Pentacles:** overwhelm the paperwork/to-do list; too much to manage. Chart crashes. Struggles to learn. The student fails to meet goals, reach deadlines and grasp the job.
- **Three of Pentacles:** Issues related to work or profession. Disputes with supervisor or subordinates. Faults, mediocrity, low production and shortcuts. Lack of work.

- **Four of Pentacles:** Refusing to let go of capital. Uncomfortable beyond the comfort zone. Mental and physical blockades. The block of the writer. Obstacles and delays. Late instalment charge.
- **Five of Pentacles:** A turning point. Slightly changed condition. Connection to the network and assistance. Or the stuff goes from bad to worse. It Occurs the unimaginable. Loss of it all.
- **Six of Pentacles:** Profiting. Claimed on false pretenses. Greed, envy, quarrelling over the property. Insurance which refuses to pay. Insurance lacuna. Unpaid loans, or mortgage redemption.
- **Seven of Pentacles:** Poverty, skills shortages. Feeling the machine let down. Charging frustration. Lack of motivation. Laughter and late.
- **Eight of Pentacles:** Keep in a dead-end job. Run-on a line at a factory. Skills underestimated. Over-qualified for jobs.

Boredom and tedium, in general, at work and in life.
- **Nine of Pentacles**: Goals accomplished but not as fulfilling as expected. Trapped in an ornate cage. Looking for a road out. Need some challenge. Too little workout. Enterprise deficit.
- **Ten of Pentacles:** Family Rejection. Disputes over land or inheritance. Controversies within the family. They Felt like an intruder. Relative elderly needing treatment. Devalued or lost Equity and assets. Losses Gambling. Material confusion.
- **Pentacles page:** Lost interest in the school or college. Bottom-up and unanswered questions. Of course, hating your decision. Worried about material possessions and appearance. Stress and fatigue resulting from overwork.
- **Knight of Pentacle:** Workaholic or it's opposite; work-shy and lazy. Obsession with a single individual or subject matter.

Weight issues, lack of exercise, chronic fatigue. Bore. Socio-inept.

- **Queen of Pentacle:** Highly home-starved, or highly Slovene. Possessions mean more than just humans. Hoarder, or set on products made by designers. Parenting by helicopter. More concerned with the success of babies, than with their well-being. Doubt, despair.
- **King of Pentacle:** Exploitable, greedy or inefficient boss. Misuse of money and power. Citizens are exploited for money or personal pleasure. Fraud: Fraud. Overeating, indigestion, gout and rheumatism. Careless for other people's interests. In family unloved.

Part 4: Curiosity

4.1 Numerology and Tarot Cards

Numerology and Tarot are both philosophies of antiquity. Numerology is centuries old, and Tarot itself is a relatively old activity. They share some similarities, although they are separate philosophies. One distinction is evident is that tarot cards have numbers in the Minor Arcana, and those numbers are based on numerology concepts. Tarot and numerology work together to produce an accurate possible reading. Regardless of that, a reading of tarot numerology will provide insight into the aspirations, hopes, and dreams of an individual.

How are Numbers Read?

To read the numbers, and to grasp the relation between numerology and Tarot, a few basic rules must be followed. It's very easy and straightforward in the Minor Arcana; aces equal one, and then numbers the cards. Tens can depend on either a zero or a one. A Tarot reading of numerology is easier to understand when considering the significances mentioned below. Digits are rolled together into a single number in Major Arcana. These rules help to bind the Tarot and numerology together. We discussed the numbers meanings in details in the previous part.

4.2 Astrology and Tarot Cards

There is no doubt that astrology and Tarot are closely linked. These philosophies apply for guidance to the astral realm. While zodiac signs and readings concentrate more on planets and their place in astrology, Tarot focuses on the astral world's supernatural force. The mixture of astrology and Tarot allows tarot practitioners and readers to expand their work, while both philosophies help improve their lives for clients. Some assume that astrology pertains to any card in the tarot deck. Find out the connections between Tarot and astrology here.

The Real Connection

Astrology plays a vital role in tarot card perception and meaning. The tarot distribution also resembles a constellation. With the advent of the Golden Dawn Order, an ancient order that was closely connected with astrology and spirituality, one of the most significant connections between astrology and Tarot was established. As a result of this order's research, many decks have arisen including the Thoth tarot, the Golden Dawn tarot, the BOTA tarot, and the Rider-Waite-Smith Tarot.

What is the difference between Astrology and Tarot?

One thing dissimilar about astrology and Tarot is their credibility. Astrology is calculable and has a close association with mathematics. In the days of the Roman Empire, mathematicians called astrologers. As such, astrology makes people feel comfortable because it is calculable. On the other hand, Tarot has its interpretation and meaning, so it is always different according to the reader. Tarot's very essence is free interpretation, and the words are taken from coincidental circumstances. Some people believe a scientifically measured astrological reading is far more reliable and has a better basis than a tarot reading.

The Zodiac: Astrology and Tarot

According to both tarot and astrology believers, each of these zodiac signs is connected to a Major Arcana tarot deck. Astrology and tarot cards are related as follows:

- Aries is connected to The Emperor, a loyalty card and The King of Wands.
- The Taurus card is the Hierophant, reflecting intelligence and finding higher truths.
- Related to The Lovers, Gemini reflects the same dual nature of choosing between high and low paths.
- Either Cancer or The Chariot portrays the joy of being safe and solving the problems of life.
- The card of Leo is Power, reflecting the strength and bravery of mind, physical, mental, and spiritual.
- The Virgo is connected to The Hermit, which is a desire to slow down and reflect on life's meaning.

- Libra's card is Justice, a state of mind in which people put their thoughts and desires aside to make a fair decision and a fair result.
- Scorpio is connected to Death, and this symbol encourages transition and change.
- Sagittarius and his counterpart Temperance is a skilled mediator and always finds its way through difficulty.
- Related to The Devil, Capricorn urges people to focus on negativity and change it to confidence.
- The Aquarius card is The Star, which focuses on hope and makes those around them feel that everything is possible.
- Pisces The parts are bound to The Moon, a creature with continually shifting moods.

It was not until later that the Tarot appeared, with divinatory interpretations in the fourteenth century. For thousands of years ago, many people used tarot cards differently. The Tarot cards were used for communicating with higher forces in cultures. Still, the tarot cards are connected with a higher self: an endless, similarly optimistic outlet helping to boost your emotional journey.

Is the Zodiac Equally Represented in the Tarot Cards?

Not all of the zodiac signs have an equal number of corresponding cards. That's because the tarot cards read a lot of energies and connect with various flows of your life's journey. Taking into account what is present and the overall feelings as those cards make themselves apparent to you. We are all able to love and relate to our higher self; people who read Tarot do the shadow work for you. Providing yourself with these internal and external random collections of choices, it often seems like the exact one you need to hear is making itself apparent. Rather than we know, astrology is broken down into so many pieces of our lives. When we immerse ourselves fully in our birth map. We can see and hear about the planet that fell on a particular astrological sign that was aligned at the birth of the second. We will know the effect this will have on us in our lives.

Inter-relationship of Tarots and the Planets

Cards represent seven solar bodies from the Major Arcana.

Mercury – The Magician

Moon – The High Priestess

Venus – Empress

Jupiter – Wheel of Fortune

Mars – The Tower

Sun – The Sun

Saturn – The World

Each of the planets represents various portions of our lives. They flow in a divinely natural way when deciding how Tarot and astrology are related. Three planets influence us more than the others:

Mercury stands for contact, the mind, all intellectual things. The Virgo and Gemini govern Mercury.

Venus, ruled by Taurus and Libra, represents passion, affection, fashion, elegance.

Mars, governed by Aries, reflects violence, sex, action and passion.

These first three planets in our charts transit the most from any other planet. They have a more direct impact on us. Often named growing challenges that we face throughout our lifetime are the larger planets throughout our charts that go into transit over the years.

Sagittarius governed by Jupiter and symbolizes prosperity, development, abundance and understanding.

Saturn stands for the law, and constraint, Capricorn governs it.

Uranus is ruled by Aquarius, symbolizing chaotic changes and revolt.

Neptune is regulated by Pisces and stands for visions, intuition, and delusions.

Eventually, we have the Pluto plant in our charts, the Scorpio sign rules Pluto, and it symbolizes change, strength, Death and evolution.

Such plants further away from us still influence us, their symbolism is unique to our journeys if we can use divinatory methods to bind them. Each astrological sign has the qualities that bind them to Tarot when we make the connection when we best understand the bond between the two. For example, Mercury rules the way we talk, think and process knowledge. Anyone in Taurus with their Mercury probably doesn't speak much, but when they do so logically and come from a steady, realistic position. It is correlated with the Taurus sign, and patient velocity is constant. Although someone may come across as too emotionally invested or too dreamy about what they're dreaming about with their Mercury in Pisces.

Table of Correspondence

Throughout history, researchers have attempted to explain the universe by categorizing it. Magicians, monks, shamans, astrologers, and philosophers were the first scholars in the natural world. They classified things in ways that make sense to them; by relating them to other items in the natural world, and by their magical and medicinal applications. Those are the foundations for modern correspondence tables. Many objects were categorized according to the signature theory, which gave value to a thing's outward appearance, others categorized items according to their attributes, and associated them with the planet's characteristics. Later, elementary correspondences inherited the properties of the planets they were aligned with, and correspondences were allocated accordingly as new objects were found and added to the magical formulary.

Correspondence tables present us with a magical-energy classification model that allows us to see energetic relationships between objects. In general, they are charts showing the relationships between different objects that have an energetically similar character. In their most basic level, such correspondence tables enable magic users to make fast decisions about spell ingredients, timing and symbolically grouping various objects according to their Intent, or, more generally, the most closely associated planetary or elementary energies with their purpose. In the 1700s, Linnaeus classified plants and animals by their reproductive characteristics and brought in our modern methods, which are also useful to learn, particularly for wild crafting and plant identification. At Herbs Listed by Botanical Families, you will find herbs classified according to the Linnaean classification scheme.

Tables of correspondence remain important for magic users today. They allow us to quickly lookup which objects contain energy that corresponds to the purpose of working our spell. As there are many different rituals and many different ways to look at magical energy, you may find tables of correspondence varying. You can find that you look at the correspondence ascribed to an object according to one source, and find it doesn't sound accurate to you. In reality, each of us has our own unique experience, and maybe not that which is representative of one person to another. If you disagree with a correspondence you wrote, try to decide what prompted it. (I try to clarify the reasons behind planetary and elementary page correspondence connections to help you with this.) If you absolutely cannot agree with your source, go with your heart.

Each planet or entity in the Western correspondence system symbolizes a set of properties. Plants and crystals are then grouped simply under the headings of certain planets and elements ideally suited to their natural characteristics. It is not so different from modern Linnaean taxonomy except that the Linnaean taxonomy primarily focuses on how the plant reproduces and thus combines plants into categories based on evolutionary relationships which are combined into groups based on supposed energetic similarities by the Western correspondence system. Gemini is governed by air (and Mercury) because it is associated with things like air (and Mercury), such as contact, looking for information and travel, and Taurus is governed by Earth (and Venus) because it is associated with things like fertility and rising things. Remember how vital your expertise and experience are and how they can make others productive. Sell your expertise as a knowledge and services guide, tutor, counsellor, consultant, manager, and teacher for others. Emphasize your experience and your consistency. Long-term strategies can support you and your colleagues; you are excellent at evaluating and managing this knowledge as well as keeping the course.

Conclusion

Tarot reading is a practice to get insight into the past, present or the future by forming a question and drawing a card. Tarot reading has its roots to the modern era from ancient times through different cultures and different ways. People believed in fortune telling in the past and still do. If you want to be a right tarot reading person, you must know about its history and its basics for reading. Tarots have different layouts including Three-card spread, Seven horseshoe spread, Astrological spread, spiritual spread and Celtic Cross spread etc. Tarots tell you about the challenges you faced in the past, the difficulties you are facing currently or the things in your way in coming days. You cannot only read tarot cards for yourself but for the others too. The first thing you need for a tarot reading is having a sacred place to do it without interruption. After that, you choose the deck of your choice.

Tarot deck consist of 78 total cards, of which twenty-two are major arcana cards, and fifty-six are minor arcana cards. They are then further broken down into four suits. Tarot card four suits have cups, pentacles, wands, and swords. Each suite is equipped with four court cards: page, knight, queen and king. There is also one ace card in each suit and nine pip cards numbered from two to 10. If you are well familiar with all these cards, you can easily do a tarot reading. If you trust your intuition, you can make the best interpretation of cards. Different symbols are attached to cards depicting you of different situations. Being a tarot reader, you need to learn the meaning of numbers and colors of each card. You will be known to the connection between astrology and tarots and how the modern tarots are like. You only need to trust yourself, when reading a card then no matter either it's a good card or bad, you can interpret it in a right way by looking at positive aspects associated with every card. Always give worth to your expertise to thrive your business.

References

- (2020). Retrieved from https://www.golden-dawn.com/eu/displaycontent.aspx?pageid=104-aims-purpose-of-golden-dawn-order
- Garden, H., HowStuffWorks, Science, Myth, & Perceptions. (2020). How Tarot Cards Work. Retrieved from https://science.howstuffworks.com/science-vs-myth/extrasensory-perceptions/tarot-card.htm
- 5 Tarot Card Spreads You Should Try. (2020). Retrieved from https://www.learnreligions.com/tarot-card-spreads-2562807
- Conceptz, K., & Allard, K. (2020). How to do a Tarot Card Reading For Yourself - Do's and Dont's. Retrieved from https://tarotavenue.com/reading-for-self/
- The Major Arcana Tarot Card Meanings. (2020). Retrieved from

https://www.tarot.com/tarot/cards/major-arcana

- All About Minor Arcana Tarot Card and Their Meaning | Tarot Life Blog. (2020). Retrieved from https://www.yourtarotlife.com/blog/tarot/minor-arcana-tarot-cards-meaning/

www.ingramcontent.com/pod-product-compliance
Lightning Source LLC
Chambersburg PA
CBHW071855160426
43209CB00005B/1069